BOLD SHALL I STAND

BOLD SHALL I STAND

The Education of Young Women in the Moravian Settlement at Ockbrook since 1799

by **James Muckle**

Ockbrook School
Ockbrook, Derbyshire

© Ockbrook School 2000

All rights reserved. No reproduction, copy or transmission of this publication may be made without written permission

First published 2000 by **Ockbrook School, The Settlement, Ockbrook, Derby DE72 3RJ**

Printed in Great Britain by
Antony Rowe Ltd, Chippenham, Wiltshire

Design by Midlands Arts Marketing 0115 948 3344

British Library Cataloguing in Publication Data.
A catalogue record for this book is available from the British Library.

ISBN 0 9536600 0 1

CONTENTS

List of Illustrations	vi
Preface and Acknowledgements	ix
Chapter 1. The Early Years	1
Chapter 2. Through a Glass Darkly. 1819-1874	24
Chapter 3. Forty peace-time years. 1874-1914	39
Chapter 4. War, Peace and War Again. 1914-1945	59
Chapter 5. Progress and Expansion. 1945-1974	85
Chapter 6. Into the Modern Age. 1974-1999	107
Pupils at Ockbrook School in 1999	125
Teachers at Ockbrook School 1799-1999	131
Bibliography and Sources	135

ILLUSTRATIONS

Minute recording the decision by lot to open the School	2
Moravian Sisters' dress, early nineteenth century	6
The first home of the Girls' Boarding School	11
Sister Ody assures the public of the continued existence of the School	21
Publicity for the two schools in the 1820s	26
Drawing by an Ockbrook girl, Margaret Watson, 1836	29
Sister Lydia Liley	31
The Settlement in 1840	36
Miss Osborne with pupils	40
Ockbrookians take tea in 1897	45
Miss Eleanor Osborne	46
The schools advertise, 1902	47
Title page of the School Magazine, 1908	50
Miss Harvey and pupils	52
Morning drill, early 1900s	54
Miss Mary Harvey	55
The School in the 1920s	58
Miss Elizabeth Titterington	61
Wounded soldiers recover at Ockbrook, c. 1916	64
The gymnasium in 1920	65
The staff in 1919	67
The School between the wars	68, 69
Larry	72
Evening prep, 1931	76
Wartime drama in daylight. *A Midsummer Night's Dream*, 1942	81
Miss J.F. Orr	83

Miss Elise Birtill	85
Little Women, 1945	89
Competitors on Sports Day in 1947	91
Tennis players, 1946	98
Physics laboratory, 1960s	99
Miss Lois Parish	100
Dr A. J. Lewis	102
Miss Driver and Christopher Neame at the 1975 School fête	109
School life in the 1970s and 1980s	112, 115, 118, 119
Miss Beryl Driver with senior girls	115
Dr Myra Rennie	116
Morning assembly in the Church, 1980s	120
Miss Denise Bolland	121
HRH the Duchess of Gloucester at Ockbrook, 25 November 1999	123

PREFACE AND ACKNOWLEDGEMENTS

A TWO-HUNDRETH anniversary is eminently worth celebrating, both by looking forward and looking back. Ockbrook School may not be able to claim alumnae who are household names, but it has many old girls who have achieved distinction in their chosen professions as well as thousands who have lived regular lives of service to many different communities all over the world. It is these women whom we celebrate directly and indirectly in this bicentenary history. Nor do we forget the boys from our Junior Department, who for over a hundred years have made a contribution to the School before moving to other establishments for secondary education – and from there into life. At the same time we look forward with confidence to the lives our present and future pupils will lead in the next centuries.

Any dispassionate person contemplating the surviving records would probably conclude that there was not enough material to write a decent history of Ockbrook School. Nevertheless, I have tried to do so. I believe that the history presented here comprises a reasonably coherent account of the life of the School since 1799. It does not disregard the companion establishments: the various day schools in Sisters' House and the Boys' (or Gentlemen's) Boarding School. Ockbrook School started as a boarding establishment: it still is one, though the boarding element is now a very small part of its work. It arose out of the belief of the Moravian Church that education, and education for young women in particular, mattered; this belief has not wavered, and the Church maintains its commitment to the ideal. The School has adapted itself to societal and educational change throughout these two centuries, and it survives as a leader in achievement and spiritual development, despite the fact that many today regard single-sex, church-led and academic education as anachronisms. This history attempts to chart the School's development as the nation's requirements for institutions and the education they offer have changed.

Readers among our old girls of all ages will scarcely be satisfied with this history. They may find their favourite mistresses ignored, many of the events they lived through passed over in silence, significant issues not dealt with. It would have been good to sift through all the records of the Moravian Church, to research the papers relating to other Moravian Schools in the hope of finding parallel material, to interview a much wider range of old girls and former staff, but time did not allow this. I plead guilty to all charges of insufficiency: this is not a definitive history and is far from the last word. I can only ask: do you know a better history of Ockbrook School? Of course, you don't! There isn't another, and if you want a better one, write it yourself! This last remark is not intended merely to scare off criticism, but to challenge some nascent scholar, perhaps a present pupil of the School, to see what she can do for the jubilees in 2024 or 2049. Meanwhile, if the story we have in this volume is only partly complete, I believe it is interesting enough to be worthwhile. It is not intended primarily for the scholarly world, but for past and present pupils of Ockbrook School who want to know a little about their heritage.

The title of this book is taken from the second stanza of the fine hymn by the great eighteenth-century Moravian, Count Nicolaus Ludwig von Zinzendorf, 'Christi Blut und Gerechtigkeit', as translated by John Wesley: 'Jesu, Thy blood and righteousness'. The words 'Bold shall I stand' seemed to convey the confidence with which a Christian education should endow young people, now as in the past, a confidence grounded not in empty self-assurance, but on the Christian principles which the School seeks to instil.

WHILE the prose in which this book is written is for the most part my own, it is good, and indeed very necessary, to thank many other people for invaluable contributions to the story. A preliminary account and chronology of the early years and of the twentieth century and some selection of illustrations was made by Miss Anne Renow. A major contribution has been made by Mrs Gail Maskalick, who placed her professional skill as an archivist at the service of the project and winkled out many hitherto unknown or unconfirmed facts from the records of the Ockbrook

Moravian congregation, especially relating to the nineteenth century. The Rev. Hilary Smith guided us through the Church archives, which she has organized into apple-pie order, and helped with her insights as a Moravian minister into the life of the Church and the Settlement. Miss Margaret Connor of the Moravian Museum, Fulneck, kindly supplied information and the original of the drawing of a chimney-sweep (Chapter 2). Mr Martin Cooke provided notes on an archival search he performed a few years ago, and he has supplied invaluable information from his forthcoming M Phil thesis: 'The Moravian Church's Anglo-German Boarding Schools and Their Contribution to Improvements in English Middle-class Girls' Education by the end of the Nineteenth Century'. Mrs Maxine Smith has produced relics from the depths of the School Library which scarcely anyone knew were there. Staff at the East Midlands Collection of the University of Nottingham, the Derby Local History Library and the Derbyshire Record Office at Matlock have all been most helpful. Dr Myra Rennie and Mrs Norah Byron provided information on their periods in office, and Miss Mary Birtill, sister of the late Head, supplied documents and photographs. Old girls, Mrs Muriel Hassall, Miss Alison Robbins, Mrs Ann Hall Pollack, Mrs Winifred Stables, and many others provided written or oral reminiscences and helped to identify persons on old photographs. Former members of staff have been very informative: Dr Ann Hope and Miss Barbara Bell. Dr Geoffrey Stead has drawn my attention to useful materials. The local historian, Miss Marion Johnson helped with her wide background knowledge of the village. Mr Gerald Hinchliffe, who was not only a governor of Ockbrook School for a good thirty years, but is also an accomplished historian of education, has read and commented on much of the manuscript. He has provided privileged information about some of the persons in the story. The present Head Teacher, Miss Denise Bolland, has taken great interest in the project and has been very encouraging. To all these people I offer my grateful thanks, but the responsibility for any errors is mine alone.

As WILL be noticed by attentive readers, I was reading George Eliot's *Middlemarch* while writing this book. I was particularly struck by one authorial comment about the truly awful Mr Casaubon, the villain of that novel: 'He dreams footnotes and they run away with all his brains.' The trouble is that scholars demand footnotes and want to know the source of, or the evidence for, every factual statement. The typical reader of this book does not, however, wish to be distracted by such things. Consequently I have decided that there will be no footnotes in the published version, but a fully annotated copy of the typescript will be placed in the School archive so that future researchers will be able to find the information if they need it.

James Muckle
Nottingham, 2000

Chapter 1

THE EARLY YEARS

THE Moravian community at Ockbrook, Derbyshire, had long wished to found a boarding school for girls. The decision to go ahead and set the school up was taken on 19 August 1798. The Elders of the Congregation met and offered prayer. With due solemnity they cast lots in order to take a firm decision. Two slips of paper were prepared. They read: 'Our Saviour approves that steps be now taken to begin a Girls' Boarding School in Ockbrook' and 'Our Saviour does not approve that steps be now taken &c.' The first slip was drawn.

The use of the lot was not uncommon in religious congregations. If spiritual leaders were uncertain about the wisdom of a momentous step, or if confirmation was sought, lots would be drawn. It was taken very seriously in the Moravian Church, but never resorted to frivolously or unnecessarily, and the rules governing its use were very strict. It was sometimes referred to as 'consulting our Saviour'. It was not to be used privately, it must be preceded by prayer, and it was not binding: the decision of the lot did not have to be accepted.

The minute book of the Elders' Conference of the Ockbrook Congregation records that the School opened on 23 September 1799, more than a year after the crucial lot was drawn, with but one boarder and five day girls. They worked under the guidance of the first teacher, Anna Pogson (sometimes referred to less accurately as Ann or Hannah).

Since they were the first in the School's history, the names of the girls are recorded here: they were Mary Anne Wakeman (the sole boarder), Mary and Sarah Holme, Nancy Langley, Anna Mary Fenton and Martha Smith. We do not know their ages. At the end of this brief history of the School we shall be able to record the names of about five hundred girls (and many younger boys too) who were the pupils of the same school in July 1999. This figure represents the highest number the School has ever had. The eightyfold increase is impressive in itself, but no-one would use it to belittle the labours of the founders and predecessors. This book contains something of what we know of their ideals and their life's work.

The context in which the foundation of Ockbrook School took place is of tremendous importance. Who were the Moravians and what did and do they believe? Why were there Moravians in Ockbrook? Why were they so zealous for the education of the young? What did it mean to be at school in those days? Did the momentous events of world history–the French Revolution, the Revolutionary and Napoleonic Wars–reverberate in Ockbrook, or were they so distant as to be scarcely relevant to the lives of the Derbyshire village dwellers of the time? Before the story of the School can be properly told, some of these questions must be answered.

Minute recording the decision by lot to open the School

The Moravian Church

The 'Moravians' derive from the Bohemian Christian reformer Jan Hus, regarded by many as the first Protestant, since he challenged the authority of the Pope and of the Church and accepted the Scriptures as his highest authority. He was burned at the stake for heresy in 1415. It was much later than this, in 1457, that certain followers of Hus formed themselves into a village community to 'adhere to Protestant ideals and live together in brotherly love, according to the example of the early Christian church', in the words of a later Moravian writer. They separated themselves from the Papacy and its priesthood and, according to the model of the primitive church, set up a ministerial order of their own.

In the centuries since then the Moravian Church, or *Unitas Fratrum* (Unity of the Brethren) has gone through many trials and tribulations. The Moravian Church is a protestant episcopal church, but a strongly ecumenical and inclusive religious organization. Its greatest eighteenth-century leader Count Zinzendorf declared Moravians were 'truly unprejudiced against their Fellow Sisters [that is, other churches], never taking part in their quarrels, never judging any Body, or its members, remaining without her Pale'. Moravian schools have for over two hundred years taken children from all religious persuasions without attempting to proselytize. The Moravians belong to a missionary church, which has taken its message of devotion to the slaughtered Lamb of God all over the world. It is a church which believes strongly in *community*–as we shall see amply demonstrated in the story of the Ockbrook congregation. 'I acknowledge no Christianity without fellowship,' said Zinzendorf. Most importantly for the subject of this book, the Unitas Fratrum attaches the greatest importance to education.

Perhaps the most famous member of the communion was Jan Amos Komenský, 1592-1670, known in the West by his latinized name of Comenius. Comenius is still today revered universally for his work as educator; indeed his ideas were not only progressive for his time, but they are modern even today. He was one of the first to appreciate that children's stages of development have a crucial bearing upon their ability to learn. Comenius can even be seen as the father of the audio-visual movement, since he strongly advocated (and published textbooks exemplifying the principle) linking words with pictures. Comenius was honoured throughout the world, came to England at the invitation of both Houses of Parliament in 1641 with a view to reforming education–a task prevented by the Civil War. It is thought he was offered the Chairmanship of Harvard College around this time. His work is highly significant in explaining the concern of Moravian communities for education.

After centuries of changing fortunes, the Moravian Church experienced a renewal in the eighteenth century. The leading figure of the Church was then Count Nicolaus Ludwig von Zinzendorf (1700-60), the 'ecumenical pioneer', as he was called in the title of the book by a distinguished former head of Ockbrook School, Dr A. J. Lewis. Zinzendorf too was deeply committed to education. He was against any coercion in schooling, refusing to countenance the forcing of pupils into a mould. His 'liberal and progressive spirit' in teaching (Dr Lewis's words again) brought him great respect among those who sought to advance the cause of education, and the concern of the Ockbrook community with schooling unquestionably reflects his influence.

Ockbrook and its Moravian Church and Settlement

Anglo-Saxons under a leader or chieftain named Occa are believed to have founded Ockbrook in the sixth century. The village appears in the Domesday Book. England was where the Industrial Revolution began, and this great change in society was felt in Ockbrook in the eighteenth century when some farm workers sought work as coal miners in nearby pits, and coal was transported through the village to the Borrowash canal.

Religious life in England in the eighteenth century was at a pretty low ebb. The scandal of absentee clergy of the Church of England, sometimes collecting a substantial stipend for doing little or nothing, is a well-known element which provoked revivals such as the work of the Wesleys and George Whitefield. Non-members of the Church of England were partly protected by the law of the land, while it was also used as a stick with which to beat them: barred from the universities, from many public offices, and sometimes from the right to baptise, marry and bury their own members in the way they chose. As late as the first half of the nineteenth century, an Anglican vicar of Ockbrook organized a public campaign *against* Catholic emancipation and treated the local

Methodists with great suspicion, while—happily—maintaining excellent friendly relations with the Moravians.

There were two consequences of this. 'Dissenters' did not see themselves as having what might today be considered a mission to the whole nation, and it further explains the need for groups such as the Moravians to settle in sharply defined communities, where they could be relatively free of interference by the guardians of civic and national conformity. It is unfortunately true that certain groups in society at this time sought to gain control of schools and enforce conformity with Anglican orthodoxy. This illustrates the need which churches like the Moravians had to set up their own schools. There *were* in fact at this time none but voluntary schools at elementary level, run by the churches and groups of church people, while secondary education, where it existed at all, was provided by the endowed grammar schools, some of which became 'public' boarding schools taking pupils from beyond their own local area.

The story of the Moravian settlement in Ockbrook goes back to 1739, when a local man, Isaac Frearson, invited an Anglican preacher, the Rev. Jacob Rogers, to preach in his barn. Rogers had been greatly influenced in London by the Moravians. Frearson clearly felt that Ockbrook was in grave need both of material and spiritual regeneration. Rogers, Anglican as he was, doubtless felt that the ecumenical spirit of the Moravians allowed him to encourage them to form a 'society' in 1740, which they did with the help of John Töltschig, who had been working in Yorkshire and had come to form a society in Nottingham as well as Ockbrook. In 1749 Parliament recognized the Moravians as 'an ancient protestant episcopal church'. In 1750 a Moravian 'congregation' was established in Ockbrook, and the foundation stone of the present Church was laid in 1751.

Bold Shall I Stand

Sisters' dress, early nineteenth century

MORAVIAN SCHOOLS

The immense contribution of Comenius and Zinzendorf to educational thought throughout the world has already been noted. It is scarcely surprising, therefore, that Moravian congregations engaged in education. The educational historian Daniel Murphy writes:

> The Moravians saw education as crucially necessary for the promotion of the way of life to which they were committed by their beliefs.

A Moravian writer in 1872 declared:

> We regard the education of youth as a portion of the work of Christ in which we have been providentially led to engage as a religious community...As settlement after settlement was established, boarding schools were considered a necessary part of the whole...If we may judge of the abundant tokens we have enjoyed of the Lord's blessing upon our schools, we have not mistaken his plans with us...

Moravians at work in the mission field needed schools at which their own children were to be educated. Members of the congregation were expected to send their children to the schools (day or boarding), which were felt to be essential for the supervision of children. The General Synod of the Moravian Church decreed in 1782 that Moravian schools were to be open to children of all denominations. Education was an integral part of church work and a vital aspect of the Church's outreach into society. In the eighteenth century there were Moravian girls' schools at Fulneck (founded elsewhere 1741 and moved to Fulneck in 1755), Fairfield (Manchester, 1785), Dukinfield (1792), Malmesbury (1793), Gomersal (1792), Tytherton (1793), Wyke (1794) and Gracehill (Ireland, 1798). The community in Ockbrook started a day school for girls in 1751 even before the chapel was built.

The girls' boarding school, the Ockbrook School of today, was therefore not the first or the only school in the Settlement. Several girls' day schools have existed there. Until 1799 they were short-lived, and they tended to operate for parts of the year only. The last of them closed in 1872 and the remaining pupils were taken into the Boarding School. Boys' day and boarding schools were founded in the Settlement in the early nineteenth century.

Moravians knew that successful schools depend on good teachers and upon financial stability. A synod at Herrnhut in 1789 resolved that teachers 'will love children, who come to see them as friends'. Children will become attentive out of love to their teacher, willingly learn what they are to learn. At the same time 'Children from their very birth should not be indulged in food and raiment, rest, exercise &c in such a manner, that an inclination to vanity and worldly convenience be thereby nourished within them; but they...should be taught to *work* as early as possible' –very necessary advice for survival in the inhospitable and harsh eighteenth century. '*Example* effects far more than *precept* or *reproof*'. 'All questions to be answered honestly.' 'Absolute obedience to God, teachers and parents to be insisted on.'

It is clear from some of the resolutions quoted here that Moravians saw it as a *parental* duty to educate their children; however, schools were necessary when parents were unable, for some reason, or incapable of performing this duty. The Moravian communities observed segregation of the sexes in living arrangements: there would be, for example, 'single sisters' houses' and the same for single brothers in any settlement. The *Resolutions* note that 'care should be taken to preserve children in innocence with respect to some things relating to human nature, for instance, the difference of the sexes &c.' Also: 'The separation of the sexes is a fundamental rule of the Congregation and must therefore be punctually observed in the education of Children.' The Ockbrook Elders' Conference minute book reports in 1795 that 'the Chapter in our Synodal conclusions relating to the education of children may be read once a year to the congregation.'

Europe in 1799

Records of the Ockbrook community and Congregation make little if any direct reference to the national political, economic and military situation at the turn of the eighteenth to nineteenth centuries. Nevertheless, mention is made of local poverty in 1806 ('business has been very black') and the financial crises in the girls' boarding school must have been due in part to the national emergency.

International events did impinge on local consciousness, at least of those who could read or who were read to from the local press. *The Nottingham Journal*, a four-page weekly broadsheet newspaper for 21 and 28 September 1799 (the beginning and end of the week of the Girls' Boarding School's foundation) devoted much space to the War. Among such items as advertisements for the sale of a windmill, an appeal for a lost black road mare, the promise of a reward for the apprehension of a 26-year-old deserter, and the announcement of two £30,000 first prizes in a national lottery, readers learn of the arrival at Calais of 23 refugee French nuns, the suppression of a rebellion in Mysore State (which at least partly frustrated Napoleonic ambition there), the campaign in the Netherlands involving Russian troops ('fine, stout, healthy fellows'), the Prince of Orange, and the Duke of York, and the presence in England of 30,000 French prisoners (while only 1,000 English prisoners languished in France–or so we are told). An item reports the looting of Frankfurt by the French during what is sarcastically termed a 'fraternal visit'! A long verbatim report of a speech by the King, requesting the right to raise more troops from the militia, is ominous in its import. A little later in the War the Moravians were exempted from military service by an extension of parliamentary provisions which applied to the Quakers.

We learn, however, on the home front that while wheat is in good supply at the Corn Exchange, barley, beans and oats are scarce and expensive. Falls on the Hamburg Stock Exchange have made money in London 'extremely scarce'. Mysore, Alkmaar, Frankfurt, Hamburg and even London are a good long way from Ockbrook, but their influence was clearly not unfelt in the quiet Derbyshire village.

THE GIRLS' BOARDING SCHOOL

The boarding school for girls was intended by the Elders to be a permanent and enduring establishment, in contrast with the various day schools. These stopped and started as the need arose. The boarding school in Moravian communities in general was to some extent intended for girls from a higher rank in society than the day schools. In 1797 a fresh girls' day school began, and it remained in almost continuous existence from then until the 1870s.

An important remark is included in the minutes of the Elders' meeting which founded the school: the Girls' Boarding School 'will be a congregational concern from the beginning'. This was normal for a Moravian school. The Elders' Conference of the Ockbrook Moravian Congregation, therefore, performed many if not all of the functions of a board of governors today. Occasionally in the history of the various schools in the Settlement the Congregation felt that influence was passing out of its hands, and bridges have had to be built. Today the Governing Body of Ockbrook School includes the entire Provincial Board of the Moravian Church in Britain, who hold the ultimate responsibility, the Minister of Ockbrook and at least one representative of the local Congregation. In line with the Church's ecumenical spirit, other 'advisory' governors from the wider geographical, educational, professional, business and spiritual community also carry the responsibility of governorship. The intention of the original founders has therefore not been lost.

The decision having been taken, the two major further steps were the provision of premises and the appointment of a teacher. The Elders, as their minutes show, did not underestimate these problems. Many, many meetings were held, particularly to find a teacher, and to persuade her to come to Ockbrook to take up the post.

Earliest Times

'We began our girls' boarding school with prayer to our Saviour for his blessing thereupon', reported the Minister in the Congregation Diary for 23 September 1799. An earlier Elders' Conference minute indicated the intention to 'begin at Michaelmas in one of the new houses'; two cottages numbered 9 and 11 adjacent to the Inn were built in 1799, and the school opened in number 11 on the street known as Shop Stones. The cottage was very small, and when a Brother Wallis died in July 1800 it was decided to move the School to his house (now no. 29 The Settlement, on Hillside). Lessons began there on 24 October of the same year.

The fees were fixed at fourteen guineas a term (£14.70 in modern money) with a one guinea entrance fee and extra charges of various sorts, including for beds. The Day School was 'at present connected with' the new boarding school, and here fees were charged weekly by subjects: reading and knitting 4d., sewing 5d., writing 6d., 'cyphering' (i.e. arithmetic) 7d. and coloured fancy work one shilling per week.

The cottage on the left was the first home of the Girls' Boarding School

The appointment of a teacher for the boarding school occupied the Elders of the Congregation for many long months. The term 'headmistress' was not used at this time, and one full-time teacher only, sometimes referred to as a 'governess', was sufficient for such a small school. Sometimes the term 'first teacher' was used, and at other times even 'manager'. At meeting after meeting names of suitable sisters were suggested and pursued. It should be explained that the titles 'Sister' and 'Brother' were used within the Moravian community for adult full members of the Church—and indeed they still are within the Church community for formal address. Some sisters were unwilling to come to Ockbrook; others were not found suitably qualified after prudent enquiry, and some were not approved by the lot; at least one was not released by the Elders of her Congregation 'in what we call a rather unbrotherly manner'. One name keeps cropping up, that of Anna Pogson.

Sr Pogson had taught in the boarding school at Gomersal, Yorkshire, and was now at the day school in Dukinfield, Lancashire. She was aged 35. For some reason the Elders of Ockbrook clearly thought she was the woman they must have.

She was perhaps a little offhand in her first rejection of the offer: 'Sr Pogson declines the proposal of inspecting our intended school–we wish she had been a little more particular in stating the reason of it'. After this refusal the Elders sought candidates in Fulneck, Gomersal, Bristol, Bath and Bedford, but eventually on 8 August 1799 the Secretary noted: 'Br Swertner informs us that at last Sr Pogson has agreed to accept the proposal concerning beginning our Girls' boarding school &c. and wishes to know when she will be wanted.' She arrived by 14 September, ten days before the School opened. Miss Pogson was paid three shillings (fifteen modern pence) a week, and this was raised to four in 1800.

Despite the energy with which the Elders had besought Sr Pogson to undertake the foundation of the School, something quickly went very badly wrong. Within two years matters had got out of hand, and the Elders' minutes report that Anna Pogson seemed 'unqualified to have the whole Management of the Boarding School'. They feared that if it could not be 'better supplied, [it] must come to nothing'.

Was it perhaps that Sr Pogson could teach the girls, but was unable to run the household? If this was so, the Elders' solution was to appoint a mother and daughter: the mother, Widow Sister Frances Sulger, to manage the School, and her daughter Elizabeth (Betsy, aged only seventeen) to be the teacher. Meanwhile, Sr Pogson moved into the single sisters' house, and in 1803 was found work superintending part of a dyeing concern in Nottingham which was owned by a Moravian businessman. If she had failed to manage the School adequately, she survived in business for 23 years; she remained a loyal member of the Congregation, though living away, and was described in 1817 as 'an elderly and steady sister' (she was only 53!) This is all the more heartening, because she had clearly antagonized the Brethren and Sisters at Fulneck by 1801 for some reason we do not know. It was formally indicated to Ockbrook that she should not return there, or she would 'not be received for some reason it is not proper to write'. Sr Pogson had some loyal friends at Ockbrook, however, and by 1826 the dust had settled sufficiently for her to return to live in a house in the Settlement; she later returned to Sisters' House, where she died on 25 July 1841 at the age of 77.

The Sulgers arrived from Fulneck on 4 February 1802, and

must have had the task of preparing for entry into a new building, as we shall shortly see. (Their name is sometimes spelt 'Sulgar' in the records.) Elizabeth Sulger's young age was perhaps not unusual for a teacher in those days, and moreover she is not referred to by the title of 'Sister' until a few years later. Betsy was the teacher, and her mother Frances the manager of the School. A letter to Br Jackson of the Settlement from George Traneker dated 20 January 1802 reads: 'Senior Sr Sulger is...very clever at her needle and an excellent housekeeper and respectable in her person, but believes that the School may be in her name, and not in that of her daughter, who is after all but a girl tho' a clever and sensible one.' Betsy was duly modest about her own accomplishments. Reading, writing, English grammar, geography and history presented no problems. 'Plain work' she could teach 'competently', but she was hoping to improve in fancy work by practice. What she positively refused to teach was arithmetic. 'It is a science to which I have always had a particular aversion, and have therefore made but little progress in it, and if Brother Jackson [the Minister] will be so kind either to undertake it himself or get some body else, I will with great pleasure do my utmost in every other branch...' She adds: 'My sincere desire and determination through our Savior's grace and blessing [is] to devote myself and my time entirely to the children.'

The Elders must have settled for this, and in fact were probably getting a very good deal. Br Church, Mr Jackson's successor as Minister ('Labourer', as it was called), is later recorded as being paid for some teaching, so he probably took on the arithmetic which Betsy could not manage. The fact that Elizabeth Sulger's salary was raised to four shillings a week in 1804 (the same as that received by Anna Pogson) implies that her work was found very satisfactory. In a minute of August 1806 her mother was referred to as 'our dear Sr Sulger who discharged her duties faithfully'. She was made a member of the Elders' Conference. It seems beyond doubt therefore that the Sulgers were held in high esteem by the Congregation. The finances of the School, however, were not healthy, and for many years the Congregation had to keep a wary eye on expenses. Almost certainly the adverse economic wartime (and later post-war) conditions continually affected the viability of the School.

Costs did not prevent consideration of the provision of a suitable building. In the very same meeting in 1798 at which lots had been drawn in order to begin the School, the intention was expressed to build a new house (known today as Liley House) between the Chapel and the Sisters' House for the use of the School. Structural alterations were made to the roof of the Chapel to allow the School to expand in that direction. The school moved to this new building on 23 November 1803. (This seems to mark a new separation between the boarding and the day schools, if certain remarks in the record are correctly to be understood, though the two schools may have continued to collaborate in many respects.) The occasion was marked by 'a cheerful breakfast attended with a peaceful feeling of our Saviour's presence.'

The Boys' Schools

At the same time, however, the Elders were not deterred from starting a boys' day school, which ran from 1806, and a boarding school, which started in 1813 and operated continuously to 1915. The boys' schools are not the subject of this book, but their existence did have an impact on the education of the girls. Some even saw boys' schools in general as a threat. The fear sometimes exists that school governors or managers, if shared by boys' and girls' institutions, might devote more funds to boys' education, believing it to be more important–this was a major problem with some of the English ancient grammar school foundations. The Elders of Ockbrook had far too much sense to fall into that trap, and it would have conflicted with the Moravian tradition.

No, the trouble seems to have been something else. As recently as 1932, in an obituary of a much more recent headmistress of Ockbrook School, the boys' school was described as 'a troublesome neighbour, as in those days boys' schools so frequently gave trouble, alas!' These words echo in the mind when one peruses the set of boys' school group photographs for 1868 to 1884 which have survived: the glowering, knickerbockered bruisers there portrayed *do* look a little intimidating. In the very early days there was trouble on at least one occasion with inebriated boys in the Church on New Year's Eve. Later in the century the unruliness of the boys gave rise to serious concern.

Maybe it was *fun*, however, for the girls to have the boys around, even if their contacts were very strictly regulated. As early as 1813 a young lady teacher in the girls' school, Margaret Collis, was reprimanded for 'an improper intimacy between herself and one of the Great [i.e. the older] boys, David Hull'. This impropriety can scarcely have amounted to much, as the conditions placed on Sr Collis's continuation in post were merely that she must 'reside in Sisters' House next vacation and dine in school'. However, single sisters had to accept the discipline of the Community, which meant that they could only choose such husbands as the Elders offered them–though they could refuse a man they had little liking for. The dénouement of the romance came two-and-a-half years later, when young David reappeared in the village, as determined to marry Miss Collis as she was to marry him. A rumpus of tremendous proportions ensued, all 'advice' to the couple was disregarded, and the Community experienced 'the painful necessity of dismissing Margaret Collis from the Congregation and the place'. Let us hope, none the less, that young Mr and Mrs Hull lived happily ever after.

The boys' schools may have been something of a mixed blessing, and the establishment of the day school probably gave rise to some minor difficulties during the tenure of office of the Sulgers. Certainly the conduct of the boys' boarding school headmaster and his wife left something to be desired in 1817, when they were habitually conspicuously absent from 'public and private meetings', a fact which gave offence to the Congregation and, of course, infringed the desire of the Moravians to be fully involved in the working of their schools. This particular matter was happily settled by tactful words between the community and the miscreant headmaster.

School Life in the Early 1800s

What can the School have been like in those early years? One may picture a winter's afternoon in the little cottage, with Sr Pogson and her six pupils beginning the great adventure of women's education into a life of cultural accomplishment by candlelight. Literacy would be achieved, but moral values, supported by the study of the Bible, would be paramount. As the afternoon progressed the candles would be snuffed, the day girls would go home and Mary Anne Wakeman would perhaps go into Miss Pogson's parlour for a simple meal.

Standards were high: a minute for 24 December 1803 notes that 'the Girls' School had a lively meeting at the break-up of School at which they produced pleasing specimens of their improvement in learning'. From Elizabeth Sulger's letter quoted above, we know what the basic curriculum was. By 1812 music had been added, and it is reported that in 1816 the Ockbrook girls participated in a performance of an oratorio on Noah and the Flood written by Mrs Elizabeth Mary Bates, a prominent, wealthy and generous Moravian of the time. In 1816 a potential teacher was rejected partly because of her lack of experience in drawing. The 'fancy work' practised certainly included lace-making, and must surely also have included the embroidery and fine white needlework with which the Ockbrook Sisters had clearly made an outstanding reputation. They were later commissioned to make a dress for William IV's consort, Queen Adelaide. Mrs Bates is credited with publicizing the high quality of this work through her friendship with prominent people in London. All of this indicates that the curriculum at Ockbrook was a good deal broader and probably more interesting than that of the grammar schools of the time, whose task it was to teach precisely that: grammar–Latin and Greek grammar. A devastating legal decision in the Court of Chancery in 1805 made it illegal to pay a teacher in the grammar schools to teach anything but the classics: modern studies had to be charged as an extra.

It is important to stress that Moravian educators believed they 'should never exchange a sound and useful education in fundamentals...for anything...which is not thorough'. How were the subjects taught in the early days? It seems highly likely that Elizabeth Sulger had been a pupil at Fulneck. She was, as we know, very young, but must have learned her lessons well in order to be considered for the post at Ockbrook. It must be assumed that she used the methods which she had experienced in her own schooling. Anna Pogson and the later governesses almost certainly used the same methods, as Moravian teachers throughout the Province met regularly to discuss their work. Comenius had urged that teaching should be as interesting as possible; the tradition of the age was none the less strong on rote learning. The best academies taught the early stages of reading by battledore, also called a 'horn-book'. This was like a small racket (as used for sports in which a ball or shuttlecock is struck) with all the letters of the alphabet in capitals on one side and in lower case on the other; the Lord's Prayer was also usually inscribed on the battledore. Miss Pogson or Miss Sulger would hold it up and invite a pupil to point out individual letters. When it came to writing, sand trays were the latest thing in educational technology: children would trace the letters in the sand which covered the bottom of the tray before being allowed to write on a slate, or eventually a piece of paper. Much effort would be expended in copy-writing. The alphabet was frequently sung or chanted, as were arithmetical tables.

The main reason for learning to read was to be able to understand the Bible. The girls would be expected to learn to read thoroughly; the Bible was a principal reading book. Verses and whole psalms would be memorized: this was still customary at Ockbrook in the twentieth century, as we shall see in Chapter 4. There were other reading books, full of high moral injunctions: none of your 'The cat sat on the mat', but rather 'It is a sin to steal a pin'. In other Moravian schools, and we can assume that teachers at Ockbrook did the same, reading was given to be studied at home or out of class, and poetry was learned and recited fortnightly.

Betsy Sulger, having declared her aversion to arithmetic, left this to Br Church. He and Sr Pogson would have taught addition and subtraction in the early stages using the abacus; sums would be done later on a slate.

In subjects like history and geography there would be a great deal of reading aloud, discussion of what had been read in class or at home, and a lot of attention given to the skill of note taking. There may have been also a great deal of rote learning, though the main stress was on understanding, and indeed there are cases in the nineteenth century of Moravian teachers being criticized for concentrating too much on memory work. A welcome relief came when the principal visual aid was used: the globe. The 'use of the globes' was a specific skill in which certain teachers were expert. At Fulneck Moravian School the girls were reported at this time to regard the use of the globe as 'a favourite occupation': Comenius, that great proponent of the visual element in education would have been delighted! Anna Pogson, Betsy Sulger and their successors had probably been taught to calculate the rising and setting of the sun and its declination and amplitude in relation to the globe.

Languages came to be regarded as very important for ladies, but French was not offered at Ockbrook until after Elizabeth Sulger's time, and then as an extra.

From a document in Derby Local Studies Library which we

tentatively date to the 1820s, we learn that drawing, music, fancy work and now French were at that time offered as extras. The girls' core curriculum included astronomy, the use of the globes and composition. This list of subjects is demanding and academic by early nineteenth-century standards, and it follows a similar pattern as was offered to the young gentlemen in the boys' school. The boys did not do plain and fancy work; they did mathematics as well as arithmetic. They also all learned Latin and could do Greek as an extra, but the Classics were in those days not offered to the girls.

Nevertheless, one great attraction of Ockbrook Ladies' School, as it was usually known, was this serious curriculum. Moravian education comes from the Continent, from Comenius's ideas via the good solid German tradition, and the parents of girls, if they cared that their daughters should be offered a challenging course of study, were willing clients of schools such as Ockbrook, which continued this tradition. It would certainly not impress those parents who thought their daughters should be given drawing and music, needlework, deportment and very little else. One textbook of arithmetic, written by a woman for use by girls and found at Fairfield Moravian School in 1804, includes a sum in which the pupil is asked to calculate how much to charge in order to make a profit on the import of a boatload of Barbados sugar, bearing in mind the cost of purchase, shipping, customs duty and the like. Such practical exercises were rarely given to girls elsewhere at the time.

Teachers were often trained purely by being encouraged to stay on in school as pupils until they were deemed qualified by reason of their knowledge and experience. In some Moravian schools promising girls were probably used as pupil-teachers. Some such girls visited Moravian settlements in Germany both to absorb the 'spirit of the congregations' there, and to make themselves fluent in German and French.

Moravian teachers, at their biennial Provincial Teachers' Conferences in the early 1800s, discussed and reviewed textbooks for study in their schools. This manifestation of in-service training must surely have stimulated the production and refinement of teaching material of various types, including the arithmetic book described.

The girls attended the Moravian Church on Sundays, and often were allowed to go to other week-night meetings, particularly the

Liturgies on Friday nights. Special children's services were organized from time to time, and in 1821 church meetings specifically for children were instituted at Ockbrook.

Discipline might have been strict, but it was intended to be reasonable. The girls would call their teacher 'Madam' in class, but 'Sister' outside. Corporal punishment of children was only very reluctantly carried out in the Moravian tradition, and the attitude was: children are reasonable beings and must be treated as such, and trained to respect one another and grow into good and useful citizens.

Play was not by any means ruled out, though organized sport entered the curriculum much later. (Comenius disapproved of competitive games.) In 1804 the girls were asked to confine their games to the walkways in front of the Church, as the grass was being damaged by being trodden on.

Work Continues, but War and Crisis Take their Toll

For a few years the School progressed happily under the Sulgers, despite intermittent financial difficulty. Then on 24 January 1808 Frances Sulger died. There seemed to have been no question of Elizabeth taking over the running of the School, though she was asked to 'have an eye to it' until a successor was found. She was still only 23. Energetic efforts began and continued to find a new first teacher, while a Sr Cox filled the temporary gap. Nevertheless, Elizabeth Sulger was granted a present of five pounds, nearly six months' salary, as the School had been so well run financially by her mother in 1807.

The vicissitudes of wartime finance are well illustrated by the ups and downs in the monetary fortunes of the schools at Ockbrook, which did not cease with the Battle of Waterloo in 1815. The Girls' School's problems were partly due to wild fluctuations in the numbers of boarders: four in 1800, fourteen in late 1803, nineteen in 1809, seventeen in 1810, only eight in 1817, ten in 1818 and fifteen in 1820. The sixty pounds' surplus achieved by Sr Frances Sulger in 1807 became a deficit of £87. 7s. 7d. in 1811 and £173. 12s. 4d. in 1817–a staggering disaster by modern standards. A salary of 4 shillings a week was paid to Elizabeth Sulger in 1804, £5 14s. a half-year for her in 1807. By 1820 women teachers were still being paid only £10 per annum; the Congregation obviously felt this was not enough, and raised it to twelve guineas (£12.60 in modern currency). Yet in the same breath, when the Girls' School was still in financial difficulty in 1821, it was suggested that this small salary should not be paid in full. Then in 1822 we happily note a credit balance of £37. 14s. 4d.

It was not until December 1808 that the Elders were able to appoint a new First Teacher, Ann Templeton. Two years later she was made a member of the Elders' conference. Poor financial results at the time did not prevent the Elders improving the premises (a new wash-house in 1812), while at the same time putting up the rent. Another difficulty faced by the School was a high level of local crime: 'disturbance in the neighbourhood and robberies'. To make things even worse, the Moravian Church nationally was worried about 'too much of a spirit of the world discerned in our schools', and while this remark must not be taken as referring to Ockbrook specifically, the local Elders resolved to communicate this concern to the teachers in their schools.

Not everything was black, however. The Ockbrook schools had an important benefactress in the person of Mrs Elizabeth Bates. Not only did Sr Bates produce funds when times were hard, but she used her financial clout to bring recalcitrant teachers to heel of behalf of the Elders. This was not just a case of a manipulative and interfering rich woman throwing her weight about. The minutes show that she was punctilious in seeking the permission of the Elders' conference to bring effective pressure to bear, particularly on the boys' school head and his wife. It is true that her benefactions were largely to the Church and the Boys' School, but her generosity undoubtedly affected the whole religious and educational community at Ockbrook.

Secondly, along with other Moravian schools in the worldwide community Ockbrook was a pioneer in the involvement of parents in the schools. The medieval tradition in education was that parents handed over their children to the teachers in boarding schools and relinquished almost all authority and responsibility for them and the way they were treated. This survived the centuries almost into the modern age. Children at Fulneck, the Moravian school at Pudsey, were rarely allowed to visit their parents; indeed, there was a very disturbing case in the third quarter of the eighteenth century–despite Moravian progressive attitudes–when a Moravian minister was not allowed to take his daughter away for essential medical treatment, even though another of his children had died of a similar complaint at school. However, at Ockbrook by 1816 it was apparently usual to hold a conference for the parents of the boarders at some time in the summer.

It cannot have been easy to be First Teacher at this time. Mrs Bates commented in 1815 on 'the distressed state of the Settlement'. Sr Templeton served as First Teacher from 1808. She

> **LADIES' SCHOOL, OCKBROOK.**
>
> MISS ODY, Successor to Miss Templeton, begs leave to solicit her Friends and the Public, for the Continuance of their Favors, in entrusting her with the Education of their Children; and hopes by her Attention to their Interests, to merit their Approbation. Miss O. will always consider it her duty, to inculcate the Precepts of Morality and vital Christianity, in the Minds of her Pupils.
> Ockbrook, March 19th, 1817.

Sister Ody assures the public of the continued existence of the School

resigned and moved to Fulneck in 1817. She stayed until her successor had taken over, and left on 17 March 1817.

Her successor was Mary Ody from Malmesbury in Wiltshire. The Elders had experienced the usual difficulties in making an appointment. They did not know Sr Ody. She was rejected at first as being too 'commodious' for the job. At this time the word meant 'accommodating' or perhaps 'easy-going'. Further 'minute' enquiries appeared to establish that she was eminently suitable. She was introduced to teachers and pupils as their new manager on 6 March 1817. Because of the delay in making an appointment, the rumour had got around that the School had closed on Miss Templeton's departure. The elders placed an advertisement in the Derby and Nottingham papers in which Miss Ody assured parents that the school would continue to 'inculcate the precepts of morality and vital Christianity in the minds of [the] pupils'.

21

Mary Ody, however, resigned in 1818, 'her health and spirits being unequal to the duties of her situation'. Within weeks of her appointment there had been further financial problems: trouble over the non-payment of fees and a realization that the School could not support its present establishment; the number of servants and teachers would have to be 'much reduced'. The Elders were so concerned for Sr Ody's wellbeing that they advised her to take a long visit to friends in the West of England, in the hope that her mental and bodily health would be restored.

Was the School to Continue?

The Girls' Boarding School had been in existence for nineteen years by 1818. In the Spring of that year the new First Teacher was appointed. She was Frances Bendall; she had been tutor to a local family and, although she had offered herself for the post, she was in some doubt as to whether she was fitted for the job. In fact, she herself asked for the lot to be used: 'if an affirmative, she will cheerfully come and do what she can'. The Elders would not use the lot, but Sr Bendall agreed to come on trial.

By the Autumn numbers had fallen. In view of her underemployment, one of the teachers who had been at the School since 1816, Agnes LaTrobe, was asked to participate in the sisters' needlework to occupy some of her spare time. Sr Bendall proposed at the end of 1818 that the lot might be used to discover the divine will as to whether the School should continue. Matters must have been difficult indeed.

The Elders, however, were having none of this. If Sr Bendall wanted the lot to be used to decide whether *she* should continue as 'future manager', well and good, there would be no objection. But the future of the School was not to be questioned. This was a courageous decision. The Congregation had started a school. Their first choice of teacher had been a catastrophe. Their second appointment had lasted a mere six years until the death of the senior incumbent. A later First Teacher had suffered what appears to have been a nervous breakdown. Material conditions, the seemingly endless national crisis, local problems, difficulties over recruiting suitable teachers and doubts over the demand for boarding education had been a constant bugbear since 1808. The Elders had every excuse for calling it a day and closing the school down. They had tried, and tried very hard. But no! They firmly believed: 'Our Saviour approves...' and they were men and women of faith. One vital aspect of faith is to persevere in a worthy cause, whatever the difficulties of the moment may seem to be. Persevere is what they did, and as the rest of this History will show, their faith was amply justified.

Chapter 2

THROUGH A GLASS DARKLY. 1819-1874

WE KNOW very little about Ockbrook School in the mid-nineteenth century. Many dozens of young people and their teachers lived full and, probably, very interesting lives, but they have left little trace in terms of written records. We are fairly sure of the names of all the principal governesses, but have no admissions registers for pupils. It is sobering to reflect that human life and experience can be lost in this way, unless an effort is made to write information down and, equally important, to see that the written material is preserved. The period is long beyond living memory, so no survivor can tell us what happened. No old girl of Ockbrook School before 1874 recorded her impressions, as far as we can tell. Photography was invented in the 1830s, but for very many years it was a painful business to be photographed, with long exposure times necessitating rigid, glazed expressions on the faces of the subjects–we may even call them 'victims'. No photographs of Ockbrook School survive from before the 1880s.

The records we have of the School at this time are sparse; they are often contradictory and incomplete. We have the Community Diaries, which sometimes omit reference to important matters. There are some Girls' School Cash Books and the Day School Accounts. There are also 'memorabilia of the congregation'–annual reports, often written in pious language, but containing useful information. Some glimpses of life at Ockbrook contained in these sources are illuminating. Moravian journals, the *Fraternal Tidings* and *Moravian Messenger* ran from 1850, but have little to say about Ockbrook and its schools. We have also the Census returns for 1841, 1851, 1861 and 1871. The first of these was compiled very carelessly and at least partly in pencil, making it hard to read. On one of the pages relating to Ockbrook the supervisor has written 'shocking bad', which is a fair comment on the poor standard of literacy of the enumerator. In a building described–clearly in gross error–as the 'Moravian Academy for young girls', two male teachers and dozens of boys are listed and no females at all: one is left with the impression that the enumerator could not tell boys from girls. The later censuses are more helpful, though the status of the women and girls listed is not always clear. Earlier ten-year censuses from 1801 to 1831 did not mention the names and addresses of individuals, but they were purely statistical analyses. However, there was a parish census of Ockbrook in 1821, a 'Survey of the Liberty of Ockbrook' in 1826, and a 'Valuation of the houses...in the Liberty of Ockbrook...1828', all of which mention the School and/or those who were responsible for it.

Another source of information is the various directories of Derbyshire: these were a feature of nineteenth-century life, containing elements of a street directory: lists of gentry and their residences, commercial concerns, tradespeople and lists of 'academies' and schools, along with a brief account of the characteristics of the town, village or parish concerned. These directories are often inaccurate, copying errors from earlier issues and from rival publications. Nevertheless, they often provide information which is hard to find elsewhere and which cannot be entirely discounted.

The later part of the period under discussion was within living memory in the early part of the twentieth century, and Miss E. E. Titterington, Head of Ockbrook School and a historian, recorded some facts in the School Magazine in the 1920s. While the documentation on which the remarks were based has not all survived, Miss Titterington's account can probably be relied upon in outline.

These disparate sources all provide nothing more than titbits of information. We therefore chart the outline of events, while offering some interpretation of them, which we hope will fit the facts as they can be ascertained.

WHEN the story reached 1819 at the end of the last Chapter, Frances Bendall had agreed to take on the ailing girls' boarding school and run it to the best of her ability. The girls' day school was running, and the boys' boarding school was by now established. Sister Bendall was still there in 1821, but had disappeared from the records by 1826. A short prospectus for both the 'Ladies" and 'Gentlemen's' Schools from this period invited applications for admission to be made to the Rev. Samuel Connor. Various directories from the late 1820s describe him as the Moravian Minister and 'a man of exemplary habits and character'; the Moravians are said to have a school, and Connor is given as its principal. This is only partly accurate. Mr Connor was not 'the'

Moravian Minister until 1836; he was a minister, but not the incumbent of Ockbrook Moravian Church. In view of Moravian opinions on the rigid separation of the sexes in education at that time, it is inconceivable that the boys' and the girls' schools were being run as one establishment. Br Connor, however, clearly had oversight of both schools, handling admissions, while leaving the

Terms

OF

THE SCHOOLS BELONGING TO THE UNITED BRETHREN,

AT

OCKBROOK, NEAR DERBY.

FOR YOUNG GENTLEMEN.

Entrance, ... One Guinea.
Board and Tuition, ... Twenty-six Guineas per Annum.
    N. B. Tuition includes instruction in Reading, Writing, Arithmetic, Book-keeping, English Grammar, Geography, History, Astronomy, the Use of the Globes, Composition, Mathematics, and Latin.
French, Greek, Drawing, and Music, each, ... One Guinea per Quarter.
    Entrance to each, ... One Guinea.
    Washing, ... Two Guineas per Annum.
    Vacations, at Midsummer and Christmas, one month each.
    Board during a Vacation, ... Two Guineas and a half.
    Payments made Quarterly.
    A Quarter's notice required previous to leaving School, or a Quarter's pay.

FOR YOUNG LADIES.

Entrance, ... One Guinea.
Board and Tuition, ... Twenty-four Guineas per Annum.
    N. B. Tuition includes instruction in Plain-work, Reading, Writing, Arithmetic, English Grammar, Geography, History, Astronomy, the Use of the Globes, and Composition.
French, Drawing, and Music, each, ... One Guinea per Quarter.
    Entrance to each, ... One Guinea.
Fancy Work, ... Eight Shillings per Annum.
    Materials for Drawing and Fancy Work paid for extra.
    Washing, ... Two Guineas per Annum.
    Vacations, Payments, and Notice previous to leaving School, as above.

Applications for both Schools to be made to the Rev. SAMUEL CONNOR, Ockbrook, near Derby.

G. Wilkins, Printer, Derby.

Publicity for the two boarding schools in the 1820s

teaching to the girls' school governess and other female teachers. To run the two schools together in this way had not been the custom at Ockbrook, and it did not remain the practice there for very long, but it was the way things were done at the two schools at Fulneck in the eighteenth and early nineteenth centuries. There is no other evidence at all that men were in any way involved in running or teaching in the ladies' school except on a very occasional basis, such as when the Rev. Mr Church helped out with mathematics in the Sulgers' time.

The Ladies' School was in trouble by 1825. Fees, apparently, were not covering expenses, and cuts were necessary: one sister was removed from the 'housekeeping' department. In early 1826 there were only three boarders, and the Elders' Conference was speaking of closing the School at Midsummer. The elders were considering how to provide for teachers who might be unemployed in consequence. At the same time, the congregation did not want to lose the school for good. Ockbrook was now the British headquarters of the Moravian Church (and remained so from 1825 to 1875) and the education of Moravian children, girls as well as boys, had to be provided if at all possible. Any closure of the girls' school would be temporary.

It staggered on until near the end of 1826. Br Connor reported to the elders in December of that year that he considered it should be suspended after Christmas. The building remained empty except for Miss Church–of whom we shall learn more later–and is described in the 1828 'Valuation' as 'house lately occupied as a boarding school for young ladies'.

The School may have survived in phantom form. In preparation for a temporary closure, the Rev. and Mrs Liley had been asked earlier in the year to receive the few boarders who remained into their family; whether they did so or not is not stated. But already by May of 1827 Br Connor was asked by the elders to enquire how many boarders might wish to join if the school started up again after midsummer. Br Connor was pretty fed up with the place by now, it would seem, and in August he gave up all care and charge of the girls' school. Yet in the following month Br Church was proposing plans–which were approved–to re-open the school 'by taking the superintendence of it upon himself, and procuring his daughter Sarah to be the Mistress'. This was approved by lot on 3 October. In January 1828 the Elders' Conference Minutes recorded the following temporary arrangements:

1. The School to be on Congregation account.
2. Sr Sarah Church to be the Mistress, and to receive four shillings and sixpence per week salary.
3. Br and Sr Church to receive six shillings per week for the Mistress's board and washing in their house.
4. If one or two boarders should offer, Br and Sr Church to receive the board wages, and the charge for instruction to be placed to the School account.
5. The School to be continued on this plan, till a suitable number of boarders enable us to recommence it on its former footing, when it will be given up to the Management then to be appointed.
6. The terms for full boarders 26 g[uinea]s per annum and one gn Entrance; for Day Scholars One Guinea per quarter and five shillings entrance.

This was the last major hiccough in the early history of Ockbrook School. We do not know exactly how long the School was in abeyance, but it cannot have been much more than a year, while–it seems likely–alternative arrangements were made to cover the instruction of pupils left without a school to go to. Sarah Church ran the renewed school until 1834, when she returned to Fulneck, where she had previously taught.

There was difficulty in replacing Miss Church. Was it ever easy to find a suitable governess? The 'Memorabilia' for this same year of 1834 further report that Mary Birtill very briefly occupied the post. She came from Bristol to do so as a favour, since no-one else could be found, and stayed only briefly in Ockbrook. Eventually Catherine Waiblinger was persuaded. 'Kitty' Waiblinger had been mentioned as a potential governess for the ladies' boarding school as long ago as 1801, when the Sulgers were eventually found. She had served Fulneck School for twenty years and was principal teacher there from 1799. She was past retirement age by 1834, having been born in 1770, and she undertook 'for the present' to be the governess. The 1841 census shows that Sr Waiblinger was still in office in the Ladies' School in that year, now aged at least 70. Resident with her were Janetta Fuller (20), listed as a teacher, and there were thirteen pupils aged between 10 and 15. (It should be remembered that the censuses were taken around Easter, when not all members of the school may have been in residence.)

Art work by an Ockbrook girl, Margaret Watson, 1836: a young chimney sweep

The 1841 census lists Ann Beesley (age given as 25) in Sisters' House also with thirteen girl pupils. This was the 'day' school. (The Community had a concept of a day school which differed only slightly from that of a boarding school: many of its pupils were expected to reside in Sisters' House, so to all intents and purposes they were in a boarding school.) The very first head of the boarding school, Anna Pogson, was living in Sisters' House too; she died later in the year at the age of 77.

By 1843 all was not well. 'Our Ladies' School, we are very sorry to observe, has been reduced very low, owing to several girls having finished their education and left the school. This was not due to any deficiency in their attention.' The authors of the

'Memorabilia' for that year go on to say, however, that they look forward to better times in view of the promised arrival from Fulneck of a new governess, Sr Robinson. As usual, it took the Elders a long time–six months in fact–to find a suitable candidate. They had been concerned at Sr Waiblinger's great age: they pressed her to retire and awarded her a pension. Susannah Robinson took over on 15 January 1844.

Miss Robinson remained principal of the Ladies' Boarding School, the direct ancestor of the Ockbrook School of today, until her retirement in 1873. In these nearly thirty years, directories and census returns refer regularly to there being *two* girls' schools. For instance, Bagshaw's *History, Gazetteer and Directory of Derbyshire* for 1846 names Miss Anna Holme, 'superintendent of needlework at Moravian Settlement', and Pigot's *Directory* of 1850 lists Anna 'Holmes' as Superintendent of the 'Moravian School', as well as Miss Robinson at the boarding school.

In the 1851 Census, 39 The Settlement is described as the Ladies' Boarding School, and is inhabited by Susan (sic–the rather grander form 'Susannah' has been shortened) Robinson (age given as 40–but she was probably 46), born in Ireland, Matilda Gregor (26), teacher born in Germany, Eliz. [?] Oaks (29), born in Dewsbury, and twenty-one pupils aged 9 to 18. Next door, at no. 40, Sisters' House, we find Rachel Empsall (43), born at York, teacher of writing and music, Agnes Spilsbury (25), whose place of birth is illegible, teacher of French and of the use of the globes, and fourteen young boarders described as 'scholars in the establishment', some aged as young as 6 or 7. Anne Beesley, who has now grown an e on her name and reached the age of 38 (she was given as 25 ten years previously), is still living there, and is described as 'teacher of Day School'.

The same cavalier attitude held by the census enumerators to age emerges again in 1861, when Miss Robinson is 56, having apparently aged sixteen years in ten. (More recent heads of Ockbrook do not find this entirely implausible. It is, however, explained by the fact that the earlier census gave approximate ages only.) Sister Gregor is still there, and Ellen Bush (24) and Margaret Craig (19), both Irish and both teachers of English and music, have joined her with Anna Beckman (20), born in Hanover, a teacher of French, German and music. The other establishment in Sisters' House is now headed by Mary Jenkins (60), assisted by Anne Coates (40), Anna Collis (26) and Margaret

Miller (19). The international background of the teachers is extremely interesting: as well as the Irish and German elements, we learn that Collis was born in Jamaica and Miller in Antigua. It is worthy of note that Moravians moved around from settlement to settlement, and from the mission field back home in a way that could not fail to stimulate openness to the wider world.

During the 1860s and early 1870s there were two schools existing side by side, both of them with a strong boarding element. The *Post Office Directory* for 1864 confirms this, by referring clearly to there being 'three boarding schools,...two [of them] for girls' in the Moravian Settlement. It lists 'Miss Lydia Liley, principal of the Moravian scholastic establishment for ladies and superintendent of needlework, Moravian Settlement' and as a quite separate entry: 'Robinson, Susannah (Miss), principal of the Moravian scholastic establishment for ladies, Moravian Settlement.'

Lydia Liley was born in the Moravian Settlement at Gracehill, N. Ireland, and was educated at Fulneck. She was running the day school at Sisters' House in the early 1860s. However, at some point this day school ceased operation and the Elders' Conference minutes for 10 April 1866 declare: 'New day school opened with Sr Liley as superintendent.' The 1871 Census return shows Susan Robinson (66–and doubtless wishing she could retire) in the Moravian Ladies' Boarding School, still with Miss Gregor in attendance (she died in 1873) and three new teachers: Agnes Robinson (perhaps a relation), Johanna Machtler and Jessie Buicke. Susan Robinson presided over 23 pupils. Meanwhile Miss Liley (57) lived next door with 13 pupils.

Sister Lydia Liley

It seems likely that the two establishments, while perceived as separate, were working together to some extent. Miss Robinson's Boarding School was doing well. It was full for many years, and could have taken more girls if the accommodation had been available; Sr Robinson bore the credit for reviving it after its having been 'reduced very low' in the 1840s. In 1867 the Elders' Conference minutes report that 'two rooms in Sisters' House [were to be] given up for use of school', for which the School was to pay £6. 10s. per annum, and this agreement was signed by Sr Robinson for the School and Sr Liley for Sisters' House. By this time the practice of single sisters living together in this house had all but died out. The 1871 Wright's *Directory of Derby* lists Miss Lydia Liley as 'Principal of Ivy House Moravian Ladies' School' and Miss S. Robinson as 'Principal of Ockbrook Moravian Ladies' School.' Sr Liley's school was therefore surrounded by Sr Robinson's. By 1873 a room in the minister's house was also being used by the School–we know this, because the Minister declared he wanted it back.

The *Moravian Almanack and Year Book* confirms that there were two girls' schools in the Settlement until 1873. The day school was attended by many girls who lived in Sisters' House–so, as we have established, it was in fact a boarding school in all but name. The governesses and teachers of this school also for the most part were resident in Sisters' House. White's *History, Gazetteer and Guide of the County of Derby* as early as 1857 clarifies the situation:

> The Rev. Samuel Wilson is director of the boarding schools and Miss Robinson, governess. There is also a private establishment here for the education of young ladies, in the Sisters' house, under the management of Miss Jenkins, which is distinct from the boarding school...though contigious [sic!] to it, and is regulated on the same principles.

By 1872-73 the day school was perceived to be in 'a sinking condition', as the Elders' minutes had it. At the same time Miss Robinson resigned in 1873 after nearly thirty very successful years at the Boarding School. It seems that Miss Liley was prevailed upon to take Miss Robinson's place. Meanwhile two other ladies, a Sr Webster and Sr Elizabeth Hunt took over the day school very briefly; it was then offered to the Misses Wilson, the middle-aged daughters of the Rev. Samuel Wilson, who had been principal of the boys' school earlier. They would have had to manage it financially on their own responsibility; since it could never have been viable in the contemporary situation, they declined, and the school was closed in September 1872. The *Moravian Messenger* for July 1873 stated: 'The two ladies' schools will now be combined under Sr Liley's management'. Since these dates and the tense of the news item in the *Messenger* obviously do not tally, the exact course of events remains to be established in detail.

The reasons for the decline of the day school are not known for certain. It may, however, be noted that the Moravians at Ockbrook now had competition locally. The Methodists had a day school in Borrowash, and there were National Schools (that is, Anglican establishments) in Ockbrook, Borrowash and Spondon in the early 1840s (and an associated infants' school in Ockbrook from 1848).

Miss Robinson died a mere two months after her retirement in July 1873. Miss Liley, 'befrilled and kerchiefed with dainty cleanliness', as her photograph shows, took over for a brief period. Records of the Congregation and of the Elders' Conference show that she played a prominent part in the life of the community until her untimely death at the end of 1874.

Why were there two schools, and what were the differences? The places of birth of the pupils in both schools, given in the census returns, indicate that both took girls from a very wide area, so it was not merely that the Sisters' House school admitted local pupils. We saw that, at the end of the previous century, there was a difference in the class from which the pupils of the two types of school came. The Ladies' School was just that: a school for young ladies of a higher class in society than the other. Its fees in 1872 were 26 and 28 guineas per annum. Some sources actually refer to the day school as the 'charity school', but it was charging 22 guineas–less, but still a considerable sum.

WHY were the girls at Ockbrook Ladies' School in the mid-nineteenth century and what did they *learn?* The changing character of Ockbrook village may have some bearing on the former matter. In 1801 only 61 of Ockbrook's population of 817, seven and a half percent, were engaged in agriculture, while 237 (29%) were in trade, manufacturing and handicraft. No fewer than 519 were classified as 'other', which we must assume meant they were gentry or private persons of high status. It can perhaps be assumed that this formed a favourable recruiting-ground for an academy for young ladies. However, by 1811 the proportion of private unclassified households had sharply declined–to less than ten percent–and this percentage remained constant for at least another twenty years. Meanwhile agriculture had nearly quintupled in extent, and trade, manufacturing and handicraft now accounted for nearly sixty percent. We see therefore a significant change in the composition of the village, most particularly an exodus of high-status families. While agriculture had declined by 1821, trade etc. made up for the deficit, and the social composition of the population remained stable at least until the 1830s.

We now take a brief look at education in general, particularly that of girls, in the nineteenth century. In England the State paid no attention to education whatever until 1833: even elementary schools, as they were then called, were purely a matter for voluntary initiative and charity, and it was the churches which undertook this work. Apart from the teaching of the three Rs, the establishment of serious education for girls was not a straightforward matter, and required positive action by determined women and their male allies. Conservative attitudes in society could not see any point at all in educating women beyond a basic level. In general, education was perceived by many in instrumental terms: what education did people (men or women) need? Boys, it was thought, should be educated for work–but not 'above their station'. If a woman was destined for marriage, childbearing and domestic pursuits, why did she need to be educated? Some regarded schooling as too demanding for women, who were sometimes seen as too stupid to receive education. A paper read to the Social Science Association in 1862 which advocated granting university degrees to women was received with 'universal ridicule'. The proprietors of girls' schools were apt to receive protests from parents on the grounds that the education being offered to their daughters was too thorough! It was clearly unladylike to know very much about anything; there were men too who did not want clever wives. To be married to a 'bluestocking' was a fate they did not relish. Many, indeed, regarded women's education as a joke. The success of Gilbert and Sullivan's *Princess Ida* is a case in point. It is significant that much of the joke in the operetta is based on the assumption that education for women is incompatible with love and marriage.

In response to these attitudes, which seem ludicrous today, establishments did exist which provided education of a sort for young ladies whose aims in life were not the selfless pursuit of knowledge or a career. A character in George Eliot's *Middlemarch* 'was admitted to be the flower of Mrs Lemon's school, the chief school in the country, where the teaching included all that was demanded of the accomplished female–even to extras, such as the getting in and out of a carriage.' As we shall see in the next chapter, deportment was important to at least one later head of Ockbrook, but the thorough curriculum demanded by Moravian educational philosophy was never neglected. The Moravian schools, in fact, provided a challenging curriculum to girls and thus were among the leaders in the field of women's education.

The Girls' School cash records contain some detailed accounts showing the books bought by individual pupils in 1849. The most frequently purchased book was entitled *Children's Guide to Knowledge*; others included Murray's *Grammar*, Curwen's *Psalmody* (probably the most successful primer of musical literacy in the nineteenth century), *Scripture and Universal History*, *Roman History*, Saul's *Arithmetic*, Watt's *Scriptures*, various geography books and a *Chronology*. The last named cost nine shillings (45 pence today), a very large sum of money at the time, when most of the others were priced around half a crown (twelve and a half pence). The sciences do not appear; nor does any branch of mathematics other than arithmetic, but in this respect Ockbrook was typical of its age.

Assessment was by public examination, that is: oral questions would be posed to the pupils before an audience of parents and community members. A minute of 1825 records that 'female teachers must never be compelled to examine against their inclination'. A later note of 1837 indicates that members of the community, both Sisters and Brothers, held a special meeting to encourage 'teachers in our schools and others employed in the service of children...for encouragement in the performance of their important duties'.

The Moravian schools were not denominationally exclusive; from the early 1790s they had been open to all. One of their objectives was, of course, to provide specifically Moravian education to children of members of the congregations. For a missionary church it was also essential to provide a stable environment and good schooling for the children of 'labourers', that is of the Moravian ministers, some of whom would be working in the mission field. Until 1853 this education was offered to ministers' children from the age of six to fourteen, but in that year the Provincial Synod changed its policy and offered them the option of sending their children from eight years old to fifteen or sixteen. This was a bold policy for 1853 and further illustrates the Moravians' commitment to the notion of education.

From the meagre notes in the Memorabilia and the Elders' Conference minutes, it would appear that during her governess-ship Miss Robinson presided over a school which began to flourish on her appointment. The year 1850 showed a profit of twenty-two pounds over and above certain expenses for repairs and alterations and the purchase of a piano. In 1853 additional teaching assistance was required. Sr Robinson was seriously ill around 1858 and was awarded fifteen pounds for help with medical charges. In the same year the first water closet was installed indoors in the girls' school. By 1867 two rooms in Sisters' House were taken over by the School. The minutes record the coming and going of several teachers over these years, four of them German by nationality or with German names. The continental connection appeared to be very strong.

The Settlement in 1840, by A. M. Oliver. The Ladies' School is to the right of the church and the gentlemen's on the left behind the old oak tree

A brief, explicit, and highly significant aim of education in the Ockbrook schools is recorded in the congregation Memorabilia for 1843. 'The most important object of education...is to bring our youth to a knowledge of the truth and to win their hearts for our Saviour.'

This will come as no surprise, but what is perhaps especially worthy of note is that the whole Community was involved in the achievement of this aim. In 1843 two girls 'have been noticed and encouraged to persevere in the good way upon which they had entered'. It seems unlikely that only two girls were 'in the good way', so one wonders if these particular pupils had become reformed characters, whom it was seen as particularly necessary to encourage.

A few years later, in 1847, a pupil called Eliza Thornton died. This girl, who was from Tobago and of mixed race, had made a strong impression on the community by her exemplary character and 'attention to serious things'. She had 'exercised a mild and beneficial influence over the younger part of her companions'. The Community Diary devotes a good six pages to a moving account, written in Miss Robinson's hand, of Eliza's last days and hours. She knew she would die when pneumonia following whooping cough was diagnosed. Teachers, fellow-pupils and Eliza herself did not shirk discussion of her death; she showed a desire for forgiveness, confidence in salvation and concern for her two sisters and her friends. She particularly asked that her sisters should come to her room when prayer for her was offered. 'She was perfectly conscious to the last, frequently uttering the prayer that our Saviour would come soon.'

THESE brief glimpses are all we can find of the life lived by teachers and pupils over fifty-five years at Ockbrook School. The Ladies' Boarding School survived, and after some ups and downs was left by Miss Liley on her death in December 1874, aged 62, in a reasonably healthy position.

By this time public education in England was developing strongly. The state was entering the educational field; parliamentary grants for the building of schools were increasing rapidly. Teachers began to be trained from the 1850s by the pupil-teacher apprenticeship scheme, which opened the profession to many able working-class women. The 1867 Paris Exhibition suddenly made the British realize that they had European competitors, especially Germany, to vie with in the field of knowledge. In the 1860s over a thousand new public elementary schools were opened. In 1870 the Forster Education Act set about filling in the gaps in voluntary provision by establishing 'Board Schools'; education for all was to be compulsory from 1880. Government did not yet consider it essential to engage in secondary (as opposed to 'elementary') education, so schools such as Ockbrook had a major part to play in the provision of schooling for those who wished to be educated beyond the age of twelve. The Moravian Church was well aware of the wind of change blowing through education in the 1860s to 1880s, and by 1868 had asked its educators to participate in the debate. The following chapter takes us into the twentieth century and shows how Ockbrook–which had never been *behind* the times–became a modern school.

Chapter 3

FORTY PEACE-TIME YEARS. 1874-1914

THE PERIOD of Lydia Liley's educational activity and that of her successor as head of Ockbrook Ladies' School, Eleanor Osborne, were marked by accelerating concern for education not merely in Britain, but in many other European countries too. As we have seen, in England and Wales the Education Act of 1870 provided for elementary schools to be established throughout the country, and in the following decade the leaving age was raised to 14 (though many left earlier), attendance was made compulsory and in 1880 measures were taken to enforce attendance. Public debate surrounding the education acts of this time was widespread, and it concerned the curriculum, the obligation to send children to school, the financing of the new system, and—perhaps most bitterly argued—the role of the established church and other groups in religious instruction.

Probably of more concern to Ockbrook Ladies' School at the time was Lord Taunton's Commission which resulted in the Endowed Schools Act of 1869. While this was concerned principally with boys' secondary schools—the public and endowed grammar schools of the time—several famous girls' schools were established as a result of the Act. The Commission and the resultant Act were the first sign that the State wished to concern itself with secondary education, and they gave a clear sign that girls' education was to be taken seriously. The Girls' Public Day School Trust was set up in 1872 and between 1873 and 1891 it established thirty-six schools. Ockbrook would now have to compete with other good girls' schools. A leaving examination, which would exempt pupils from the matriculation examinations at Oxford and Cambridge was instituted, and in 1878 was extended to girls' schools; the northern universities followed suit, and soon a 'lower' certificate was introduced too. The age of academies such as Lowood school—the fictional, but ominously convincing establishment attended by Jane Eyre—was over.

Miss Eleanor Osborne was aged about 47 when she became principal of Ockbrook Ladies' School in 1874, and by 1881 she was well established with six assistant staff, four female servants and 31 resident pupils. The staff were her nieces Emma (aged 28 in 1881, and styled 'first teacher') and Eleanor (26) Lang, Susanna Boag (25: one Henrietta Boag had been teaching at the day school in 1871), Martha Keuge (21, from Germany) and two Irishwomen: Eliza Hanna (19) and Matilda Barnes (20), both of whom were described as 'junior teachers'. The connection with Ireland is further illustrated by the fact that Miss Osborne herself was born there.

Miss Eleanor Osborne (centre) from a group photograph, 1888

The spirit of Miss Osborne's rule at Ockbrook is best summed up by the reminiscences of two old girls. The first relates to the earlier part of her term of office. As it appears here, it is edited from a number of personal letters received by Elise Birtill, a later Head of Ockbrook, in 1949. The author is Ellen Parry-Jones, née Passmore.

Miss Osborne used to ask us to contribute to a wreath, or flowers, on the anniversary of Miss Liley's death.

Mr Baxter was the minister, and as the church was undergoing repairs services were held in the 'lecture hall'.

We had two dining rooms, one for those who learned French, and we were allowed to talk in French at meals; silence was the rule in the other room. Miss Osborne was a short, round little woman, but a grand disciplinarian. Whatever her other attainments were, she knew her Bible, and without having to refer to it, would deal out from six to twenty verses to be learned as a punishment according to the crime.

Things were very spartan, bare boards, backless forms, very thick bread and butter for breakfast and tea, never anything else. We got up at 6 a.m., breakfast at 8, prayers 8.30; only two baths, one upstairs for senior girls. We younger girls had our bath in the back kitchen; there was usually a good fire which we appreciated.

I was christened Nellie, but Miss Osborne said Nellie was a corruption of Ellen, so Ellen I remained.

The school year was divided into four quarters; the change to three terms was made soon after I left. There were no organized games, no facilities for tennis, netball, or hockey; there were two swings at the far end of the playground, and if you possessed a ball or skipping rope you might play with it there; mostly the girls strolled up and down with a friend.

We had about fifty boarders and six day pupils. On Saturdays an old woman (Ellen Plowright) brought in a large basket of sweets, and we could buy penny bars of chocolate, large bull's eyes twopence and a penny, red toffee cherries with wire stems for a halfpenny.

We wrote rather dreary essays on subjects like 'Disappointment', etc. This essay on 'Disappointment' I remember to this day, because I spelt it throughout with one 'p' and had to write it out one hundred times.

Among the teachers I remember a Miss Boag, Miss Walker and two Miss Langs. Miss Minna Lang taught me singing and music. I do not remember many girls except Ethel Clarkson, I think from Leicester, my chief competitor for the drawing prize, Annie Topham, who became governess in Kaiser Wilhelm's household, and Amy Cottrall.

I was not unhappy at school, made friends, liked some of my lessons and hated others, just like schoolchildren do now. I went to Ockbrook when I was nine years old in 1874 and left in 1881.

The author of the second brief memoir is Charlotte Mabel Nelson, 1877-1956. Miss Nelson was a lifelong inhabitant of Ockbrook village, but she was a boarder at the Moravian school in Bedford for most of her school career. However, she wrote these brief and interesting remarks about Ockbrook School, which she attended briefly as a day-girl in the 1880s.

Backboards were used to straighten the shoulders and passed from girl to girl during lessons, which in those days were one hour. The backboard, about four inches wide and a yard long was placed across the spine and held in position through the elbows. We sat with this for about five minutes. Each classroom had a reclining board on the floor. This was a slightly sloping board about six feet long, covered with red and green baize. On this we had to recline on our backs for about ten minutes during preparation.

A good deal of piano practice was done before breakfast.

When we filed out of the classrooms, which were also our living rooms at night, we had to shake hands with the teacher and say, 'Good-night, Miss Lang.' On leaving the dining room after meals we had to turn round at the door and curtsy to Miss Osborne and the remaining teachers. If this was done hurriedly we were recalled and had to curtsy again and got a conduct mark if it still did not please. The same was expected from us when leaving the dining room, where we had our delightful Friday afternoon callisthenics!

Our pens used in writing class had two and sometimes three little metal disks arranged up the holder in the right place for the thumb and fingers to rest, and once a term we had to write a specimen copy in our best handwriting with very ornate capital letters at the beginning of each line. These were trite little verses, the one I remember best being:

> *Tender hearted, stroke a nettle,*
> *And it stings you for your pains,*
> *Grasp it like a man of mettle*
> *And it soft as silk remains.*

Miss Osborne retired in 1889. Many of these foregoing customs were carried on for a time under the new headmistress, Miss Harvey, but gradually more modern methods were introduced.

One certainly hopes so. The modern educator finds little in these two testimonies to enthuse about. The insistence on backboards must have ensured that the girls' minds were not fully on their studies. The boring subjects for essays, the 'trite' poem for copying, the lack of healthy games except for callisthenics, the use of the Bible as a punishment, and—most of all—the lack of any sense on the part of these two women that studies in school were interesting, stimulating and worthwhile—all this leaves the reader disappointed...or should it be 'disapointed'? Mrs Parry-Jones, in a letter not quoted above, commented in 1949: 'What a vast improvement in the teaching of English, judging by the contributions by the pupils in the Magazine. I feel sure neither I, nor any of my contemporaries were capable of such efforts...' Yet one former pupil became a governess in the Kaiser's family, and Miss Nelson later in life became an inspiring teacher of art and music at Ockbrook School. It may be significant, however, that after a brief period under Miss Osborne her parents sent her away to board elsewhere.

One of Miss Osborne's former pupils was still alive—believe it or not—in 1970, aged 103. Mrs Sarah Jackson (née Brown) remembered that Ockbrook in those days was 'a good school. Very strict. No favourites. Some of girls did not like it. I was sorry to leave.' Her education had taught her a hatred of idleness: she took up crochet work at the age of 102 rather than have nothing to do.

The reminiscences raise some interesting points. To eat meals in silence seems unnecessary, though it was a well-established custom in religious orders; however, it scarcely makes it possible to teach certain aspects of table-manners. Permission to speak in French is an example of the use of extrinsic motivation to learn, and was not a bad idea. Miss Osborne seems to have had a touching respect for her predecessor, whom she almost certainly knew well, and the custom of leaving flowers in memory of Miss Liley is a pleasant one. Yet the memoirist does not seem to be very aware of what Miss Osborne's 'attainments' were, other than strict discipline and dishing out texts to learn as a punishment. The insistence on 'Ellen' rather than 'Nellie' reminds us of Mr Gradgrind in Dickens's *Hard Times*, who insists that Sissy Jupe is Cecilia—and goes so far as to instruct her to tell her father he must not call her 'Sissy'. Among the teachers mentioned, Miss Walker does not appear in the 1881 census return, and which of the two Langs was known as 'Minna' is not clear.

Financially the School was well managed by Miss Osborne; it was only in 1886 that a deficit was reported. Perhaps there were other difficulties around this time. When a little girl died in 1887, the Elders expressed their sympathy to Miss Osborne for 'the recent trying circumstances through which she had passed.'

In an obituary in *The New Star* (the Ockbrook School magazine) for 1901, Miss Nelson waxes more warmly about Miss Osborne. We learn, 'She was feared by some, loved by others and respected by all who came under her care...She always found time to tend to the educational wants of the individual...We went to her room by twos and threes for extra lessons, and many will agree with me that it must have been from her great sense of duty she did it, for it was, I fear, a thankless task.' The writer adds: 'I am sure many who lived under Miss Osborne's care can speak of the lasting effect of her religious influence upon their characters.'

Her 'religious influence'? Even that gave rise to some unease in the Moravian community. The minister, Mr Baxter, complained in 1881 that Miss Osborne was teaching Calvinist doctrine. Girls had 'remarked to him that she teaches different doctrine to what he does.' Calvinistic views have never had currency in the Moravian Church.

The further career of Annie, properly Anne, Topham, Kaiser Wilhelm II's family governess, is of great interest. She was at the School for a relatively brief period, but her sister studied at Ockbrook for longer, and four nieces were prominent members of the School in later years. By the teens and twenties of the twentieth century Anne had become a very successful author: she published six or seven novels, two of them anonymously and two under the pseudonym E.R. Rashid—an interesting *nom de plume* in itself. She issued three volumes of memoirs of her experiences in the Kaiser's family, published in Britain, America and France.

Memories of the Kaiser's Court appeared—fortuitously—on 15 August 1914 and was so successful that no fewer than ten editions appeared within a year or two. Its success was not merely due to the momentous political and military events which accompanied its first appearance, but to the fact that it is uncommonly well written. One of her books on the Kaiser's family was reissued in America as recently as 1992. This in itself makes one brief incident in the early pages of the book significant. After all, Anne Topham must have learned to write well somewhere—and why not at Ockbrook School, despite the boring essay titles? The anecdote also illustrates why the Kaiser nicknamed her 'the British Dreadnought'. In the presence of the Empress, Miss Topham allows herself an outburst, when addressed by the German language tutor of the young princess:

> '*Nicht wahr*, Meess? Is not grammar one of the most beautiful, most interesting studies to which one can devote one's mind?'
>
> 'It is the most hateful, most unnecessary thing possible,' I replied rather hastily; 'we never consciously use it when we speak, we forget it as soon as we can. I detest it'...
>
> 'Hurrah!' [the nine-year-old Princess] shouted... 'There! You see, Herr Schmidt, there *are* other people who can't bear grammar. Hurrah! I've heard the truth about grammar at last!'

One wonders what Miss Osborne would have thought of that.

Ockbrookians take tea in 1897

Miss Eleanor Osborne

Miss Osborne left Ockbrook for Bristol on her retirement, and she died there on 9 September 1901. If her 'commanding figure and grey ringlets had struck awe into the hearts of young and old alike', the young Mary Harvey must have come as a breath of fresh air in 1889 when she arrived from the Moravian school at Bedford to be head at the age of 29. Miss Osborne's appearance and deportment have even been likened to Queen Victoria's, 'a great and elderly dame' more than twice Miss Harvey's age when she retired, and into whose shoes it cannot have been easy to step. In the late Victorian era, to be old and experienced was prized above all else; to be young (and even forty was 'young' in this sense) was to be an object of uncertainty or even suspicion. Miss Nelson remarks that the backboards and curtsying were not abolished at once; Miss Harvey moved tactfully and patiently to turn Ockbrook School into a more modern and liberal establishment.

No less distinguished a figure than Sir Michael Sadler (former Chief Inspector of Schools, and professor of Education at Manchester University) carried out a *Report on Secondary and Higher Education in Derbyshire* during 1904. Coming as it does right in the middle of Miss Harvey's tenure of office in Ockbrook it provides interesting context for her work at the School, and it shows how very important schools under private management were for secondary education in Derbyshire. Over thirty percent of pupils receiving secondary education were at that time in private establishments. In the public secondary schools boys outnumbered girls four to one, but in the private sector numbers were roughly equal. The private girls' schools like Ockbrook were therefore more than holding their own for women's education, since more than half of all the girls in the County receiving secondary education were in such schools. Sadler called upon the County authorities to recognize and capitalize upon the major contribution made by schools under private management.

Ivy House was the chief building when Miss Harvey took over the School. There had been an upward trend in pupil numbers from the mid-1880s, and at last the School seemed to be on a stable footing. There were forty-three girl boarders and twelve day pupils in 1890. The fees were 32 guineas per year. The buildings soon proved too small for the fifty to sixty pupils (boys as well as girls in the preparatory department by now) whom Mary Harvey had encouraged into the School. A kindergarten was introduced, and in due course all the buildings above the Chapel were annexed for the use of the Ladies' School.

The 1891 census appears to show only three assistant staff

160 Derbyshire. Bennett's Business Directory. Ockbrook

Sims J, farmer, Burnwood
Sims S, carrier.
SPENCER J H, tailor and outfitter, Church st, and New st
Street H, baker, Green Lane
Street Mrs, gardener, Melbourne Cottage
Webb J, baker, Flood st
White Swan Inn,—G Draycott

MORAVIAN
Boarding School for Boys,
OCKBROOK.
Application to be made to the Rev. J. M. Maliálieu, Ockbrook, Near Derby.
Terms moderate. Prospectus on application

SCHOOL FOR YOUNG LADIES,
Moravian Settlement, OCKBROOK.
MISS HARVEY,   Principal.
Terms Moderate.   Prospectus on Application.

The schools advertise, 1902

who were resident and only 14 scholars, but 43 pupils are recorded in Church sources for 1890, so it may be assumed that many boarders had gone home for the holidays by 5 April, when the census was compiled. The teachers named were Sophia L. Herzberger (from Bavaria), Mary Rea (a Scotswoman) and Sarah L. Hanna (British, born in Jamaica). The Langs and all Miss Osborne's team had disappeared. It does seem that the Misses Robinson, Liley, Osborne and Harvey all brought or recruited

47

their own crew, who in the first three cases nearly all left with their captain.

The Gentlemen's School was still occupying what is today the main school building, and it continued to do so until 1915. The close proximity of the boys was a mixed blessing. Nineteenth-century boys' schools were rough and sometimes unruly establishments, and Ockbrook was no exception. Young gentlemen, whether at school or university, were expected to be high-spirited and adventurous and if they were sometimes rowdy, that was no particular surprise. The Ockbrook Boys' School song (composed by their headmaster, Ernest Walder!) conveys something of this spirit. One verse reads:

> Of precepts we have a good store,
>   And a slender acquaintance with letters,
> Of practice we might yet have more,
>   (But so might some of our betters)
> Yet with good Ockbrook fare
> And clear Derbyshire air,
>   We intend to do something in life.

Boys did not kow-tow to their masters, and at best observed an uneasy truce. The undisciplined behaviour of the boys at Ockbrook gave much cause for concern, to the extent that it was particularly mentioned in the 1890 report on the School in the *Moravian Messenger*. There was at least one case of a gifted master having to leave because of his inability to cope with the boys' behaviour. None of this was Miss Harvey's responsibility, but a troublesome neighbour can be a considerable nuisance.

Miss Harvey's academic innovations were significant. More subjects were introduced. Some of the old ones were modernized. Stultifying copy-drawing was replaced by drawing and painting from nature. Musical training took a leap forward when the School began to enter pupils for the graded examinations of the Royal College of Music and Royal Academy of Music which had been instituted in the late 1870s. Needlework, plain and fancy, reached its highest pitch ever. Awe-inspiring inspectorial visits by members of the Board of Governors, during which the girls would have been tested and interrogated, were abandoned. Doubtless the practice had led to some extent to more rote learning and rigid teaching than was desirable.

It was by no means thought necessary for pupils in any school to take external examinations. Many teachers and parents felt them to be harmful, particularly for girls, in that they encouraged 'an undesirable spirit of emulation'. In Eleanor Osborne's day, if the girls had taken any external examinations, they were those of the College of Preceptors. This body pioneered examinations for school pupils as a means to achieve higher standards in secondary education; their first examinations were held in 1850—in a school in Nottingham, as it happens. Though they were the first school examinations, they were never the most successful. By the end of the century the more demanding Cambridge Certificates were being tackled successfully at Ockbrook.

The nature of these Cambridge examinations gives us some clues to the curriculum offered to Ockbrook girls under Mary Harvey. Cambridge Local Syndicate examinations were chosen because their religious education syllabus, while compulsory, was non-sectarian and suitable to a non-Anglican school such as Ockbrook. Oxford, on the other hand, at a time when the spirit of the age was moving towards toleration and an open attitude to dissenters, was perceived as illiberal because of its strictly Anglican syllabus in religion—though, unlike Cambridge, the paper was not compulsory. Those girls who entered for the Junior Certificate would have to pass the preliminary examinations, which consisted of English (analysis, parsing, composition), arithmetic, geography and English history. They would take religion, which was based on scripture and not Anglican church doctrine. In addition they would have to take at least one and not more than four subjects from the following: a language (Latin, Greek, French or German), mathematics (Euclid and algebra as well as arithmetic), mechanics, chemistry, botany and zoology, and drawing or music.

The very few girls who entered for the senior examination were presented with four sections plus drawing and music. They had to pass two of the four, or one of them with drawing or music. The four options were English studies (a 'fair knowledge' of one of the areas contained within 'English' sufficed: history, literature, political economy or geography), a language (one was sufficient), mathematics pure and applied, and one of the aspects of 'physics' (which embraced natural philosophy, chemistry and vegetable and animal physiology).

Ockbrook girls certainly never chose the scientific options in either examination: very few girls in the whole of England did—in some years none at all. The lack of scientific education at Ockbrook was bewailed by inspectors well into the early twentieth century. Nevertheless, the teaching at Ockbrook was strong in the arts, and in view of the constant presence of teachers from the continent of Europe, languages cannot have been neglected.

Another of Mary Harvey's innovations was to encourage a school magazine. It began in 1901, and was at first known as *The New Star*. There had never been an *old* Star: the idea was to have a 'new star of the new century'. The twentieth century was clearly considered to have started, logically, in 1901 rather than 1900. The member of staff who founded and edited it for two years until she left Ockbrook was a Miss Dawes. The title had three other resonances: the Moravian symbolism of the star, an acronym for 'School of Thought And Reading' and also for 'Striving To Attain Renown'.

Title page of the School Magazine shows an Ockbrook girl engaging in a favourite hobby

Copies of this journal (except for the very first issue) survive in the School library. It was produced by the laborious 'jelly' method until 1908; before the days of modern reprographics and until about 1950 this was a common method of reproducing small-run bulletins. A jelly was made according to a recipe resembling the witches' brew in *Macbeth*. The script (in the case of early issues of *The Star*, handwritten) was somehow absorbed in negative on this concoction and was then transferred to paper in multiple copies. The results were mediocre in the extreme. Eventually Miss Harvey provided a 'cyclostyle', which improved matters somewhat.

The poor method of reproduction is not reflected in the quality of the contents, which are lively both from the literary and visual point of view. Nor did it dampen the enthusiasm of the editors and writers, who produced no fewer than nine issues in 1901.

School news, stories, poems, essays, drawings and cartoons (especially a series of pictures of school life in which girls are replaced by cats!) fill several issues every year. In 1909 no. 1 of the *Ockbrook Girls' School Magazine* appeared in fully professional printed form. In all of these periodicals news and addresses of Old Girls feature prominently.

The innovation of a magazine further emphasizes Miss Harvey's concern for the intellectual development of the pupils in her charge and the strengthening of a school spirit. She encouraged an essay-writing competition. The titles were not always of the type of 'Manners makyth man', but sometimes were more relaxed: 'Shrove Tuesday at Ockbrook Ladies' School.' *The Star* for June 1902 displayed the new school badge: red and white with an OGS monogram. 'Let every wearer of this badge, wherever she may be see to it that she keeps its honour free from the last stain of disgrace,' writes the Editor. The cover of the May 1904 issue bears a new coat of arms, designed by Miss von Flotow, a teacher who served the School for many years. The monograph, the pen of learning, a sprig of ivy and an (apparently) learned young woman form the quarterings of the shield.

In the 1890s we discover an explicit public statement of the aims of the School. To be accurate, it refers to both the boys' and the girls' schools, and, as published in Bulmer's *History, Topography and Directory of Derbyshire*, it runs: 'to afford sound and ample instruction in the various branches of learning requisite to a useful and liberal education, and to train the pupils in such a manner as to embue them with the principles of Evangelical Christianity, and to prepare them for the faithful and efficient discharge of their duties in after life.' This places the Ockbrook schools firmly on one side of a strong nineteenth-century educational controversy, between those who believed education should be secular and the others for whom the purpose of education was primarily religious.

Concern for those who studied at Ockbrook even after they left is illustrated by the contact maintained with old girls in the nineteenth century. As many as fifty-two, from what was after all a very small school, assembled in 1899 to celebrate the centenary. 'Luncheon at one in the school dining room, tea at 4.30, and a cheerful service in the chapel at 5.45.'

Mrs M. G. Shawe, an old girl and later a mistress at the School, published a few reminiscences of Miss Harvey's time in the *Ockbrook School Magazine* for 1949. Here are some extracts from what she wrote:

> Day scholars walked up from Borrowash and over the fields from Spondon, a few from beyond Elvaston, riding or being driven part of the way. Little boys came to the 'Preparatory Department' with or without sisters, and their schoolroom was the 'prayer hall', so called from Sisters' House days, and it was still used for school prayers.

Miss Mary Harvey (centre) from a school photograph of 1905

> A field was taken over, beyond the tennis lawn, chiefly for netball. Along the lower hedge were the girls' gardens, where some toiled with much zeal and pleasure, partly inspired by Miss L. Hanna's interest and example.
> In Miss Harvey's early days the Christmas breaking-up entertainment was held in the school dining-room, which was very small for the purpose, and before long it was decided to use the 'sleeping hall' instead. For this all the beds had to be removed, some to bedrooms beyond and

some to the floor below. A mighty upheaval this was indeed, and the resulting congestion was a source of great joy to the 'displaced persons', who made the most of their opportunities. Old girls of those days will remember toiling at elaborate festoons of evergreens, which were hung from the beams, and along the walls. A platform was erected—on benches—at one end, and there the girls sat, coming down to the floor in front to recite (no plays in those entertainments). The piano was all important, but just how it arrived up in the hall I cannot think. Guests then did not include many parents, partly because some lived in London, Scotland and Ireland, and partly, of course, because it was before the days of motors.

Then, as now, there was an exhibition of work done by the girls, but it was of a very different kind, being chiefly plain sewing in fine long cloth, with many tucks, back-stitched seams, and much feather-stitching, to which many hours were devoted. Miss Harvey superintended the 'fancy work', and there were some beautiful pieces of embroidery on satin and linen to be seen. There were no gay and intriguing 'crafts' in those days, until the Preparatory people began theirs.

In the nineties, the whole school wore pinafores, full ones of white muslin, with yokes of embroidery. On Friday evening they arrived in two clothes baskets, billowing with starch, to be dealt out by the 'week-doers'.

School outings were very few, and the one which celebrated Miss Harvey's official birthday (her real one was at Christmas, and so quite useless) was a very festive occasion.

In early days we went once or twice to Dovedale in Mr Simms's brake, and at Brailsford we waited to give the horses a rest. No whisking along in a motor-coach for us!

There were candidates for the Cambridge examinations, both senior and junior in those far-off days, though only a few at a time...There was much happy, busy life, then as now, and then, as now, many lasting friendships were formed.

Mrs Shawe here mentions boys: we do not know exactly when young boys were first admitted to the girls' school, though a school photo from as early as 1888 shows the odd one. In Miss Harvey's time boys must surely have been preparing for entry to the gentlemen's school next door. The day pupils were clearly very local. It is good to read of a sports field, even if fully compulsory games did not become normal until later under Miss Titterington, and of gardening as a recreation. Outings, superb needlework, festive entertainment at the end of term—though no drama. The notion of the theatre as a place where propriety could

Morning drill, early twentieth century

not be guaranteed survived for the moment. Nevertheless, the picture is pleasing. In contrast to Miss Osborne's period, 'Liberty was given instead of taken', wrote one old girl.

The same anonymous former pupil paid eloquent tribute to Mary Harvey at the time of her death in 1932. The words are of unusual warmth and convince us of their sincerity:

> Miss Harvey's influence was strongly felt. Her kindly sympathy and quick understanding toward the girls and teaching and kitchen staff left no-one in doubt of her friendship. She was just and fair: punishments did not come easily to her. Hers was, of course, the last word, and knowledge of this fact frequently obviated the necessity of its being uttered. A born nurse, no child was sick but Miss Harvey nursed her well again. Her gift of sympathy stood her in good stead here. She gained the confidence and friendship of the girls in a wonderful way...Her benign influence remained when schooldays ceased to be.

On her retirement Miss Harvey remained in Ockbrook, where these friendships with old girls could easily be maintained. She lived with her sister and brother in the house known as Broadstairs, which did not at that time belong to the school. One of her most important services to the School was that she gave it an identity which, despite all the achievements of earlier years, it did not quite have until her days. She did this through her humane outlook, her development of work inside and outside the classroom, such elements as the school magazine, the stiffening of the academic backbone of the establishment, and clear statement of the ultimate aims and objectives of the School. Mary Harvey took the first of many steps with her successors in developing Ockbrook into a modern school. There were nearly fifty pupils in the School at the time of her retirement, and the establishment was well and economically run. It is a pity that the magnitude of Miss Harvey's contribution did not always seem to be fully appreciated: the obituary published in the School Magazine when she died in 1932 was so short as to appear perfunctory, and a school gardener who died around the same time warranted a longer article. This must surely have been an isolated lapse.

Miss Mary Harvey

We have another source of information about everyday life at Ockbrook before the First World War, this time from the point of view of one of the teachers. The redoubtable Ellen Irene Low came to Ockbrook in 1912 and remained on the staff teaching girls in the Junior Department and ruling all—from juniors to prefects—with a rod of iron until 1962, when she was seventy-four years old. When she left, Miss Low published a brief but witty and entertaining seventeen-page pamphlet entitled *Fifty*

Years at Ockbrook School, which concentrated on the lighter side of school life, and which contains many details of the living and domestic arrangements and the girls' activities.

The School was then accommodated, as has been mentioned, in the houses above the Chapel, those known today as Liley House, Ivy House (which is now two houses) and Sisters' House. Miss Low reports that the top floors of these houses were used as dormitories, the largest of which was called the 'sleeping hall'. The three teachers slept in this dormitory in separate cubicles, while the girls slept in rows of beds, the rows being separated by curtains. The mistress on duty could see over the curtains and ensure that no-one was up to any mischief after lights-out. There were two rooms for washing, dressing and storing clothes separately from the dormitory. The maids slept below, and on the ground floor coal and provisions were stored. (This part of the building was pulled down when the boys left Ockbrook and the girls took over the present building, which had always been the boys' school.) Miss Low taught in the 'prayer hall', and for several weeks found the building very confusing, occasionally having to mount the stairs to the dormitory and start again in order to find whatever room she was looking for.

The bathing arrangements in 1912 were exactly the same as described by the old girl from Miss Osborne's time. It was only in the kitchen that water was hot: girls who felt themselves 'superior' would bathe upstairs, but were allowed only one bucket of hot water per bath, carried up two flights of steps by the long-suffering maid Flossie. Miss Low preferred the warm and convenient kitchen, where hot water from the copper was easily obtained. This convenience was bought at a price, however. On one occasion Miss Low was imprisoned in the bath beneath its hinged lid—the lid was, when closed down, used as a draining board for the kitchen sink—when it slammed down unexpectedly, trapping her beneath.

The daily régime began at a quarter past seven; breakfast was at eight. After eating, each senior girl had to learn two verses of scripture and two of a hymn and each junior girl one of each. They had to say them to the staff before leaving the room. 'They learnt them remarkably quickly,' comments Miss Low.

Music lessons were at 8.30, and school ran from nine till twelve; a walk before dinner followed. Afternoon school, tea, free time and evening preparation took the pupils to supper time.

They were supposed to go to bed in silence, but this rule was often disregarded.

As for school uniform, the pinafores referred to by Mrs Shawe were still worn ('of various shades of white', as Miss Low drily reports), and the girls over twelve years old wore long black stockings and skirts ten or twelve inches from the ground.

Speech Day, like the breaking-up entertainment described above, was held in the big dormitory, after the beds had been cleared away, and mattresses and bedding stacked high on used and unused beds. A platform was erected at one end. One can imagine a festive spirit on the last night with girls and mistresses sleeping in these makeshift conditions: Miss Low had to climb on her dressing table to get into bed, and could see over the curtains without any problem.

There was an annual tradition of holding a 'toffee sale' in the summer for charity: often enough for Moravian missions. This was held at the end of the summer term, and there would be a performance, 'a scene from some well-known book' as Miss Low says—so, if her recollection is correct, by 1912 to 1914 drama was creeping in. Tea on these occasions was served in the garden, and, of course, home-made toffee sold. In 1914 this was the occasion for a reunion of old girls and the presentation to Miss Harvey on her retirement of a Crown Derby tea-set.

WHEN the School broke up in Summer 1914 few can have imagined that they would reassemble in wartime; certainly no-one at all dreamed that the War would be so terrible and destructive. Many of the girls were to lose brothers and fathers; all were to endure hardship of one sort and another. An extremely long period of peace in Europe was at an end, and the next thirty years were to be desperately unsettled for everyone. Ockbrook School did not come off unscathed; we shall see that there were crises in the following years, but the School was sufficiently stable to survive and eventually to flourish.

Ockbrook

Chapter 4

WAR, PEACE, AND WAR AGAIN. 1914-1945

WHILE war was very much on the mind of people all over Europe, it was not the exclusive concern of the British population: during these years plans were being made for the future, perhaps more urgently than in time of peace.

In the early decades of the twentieth century, nations all over the world gave a great deal of thought to the future of education. In Britain it became obvious that the administration of schools needed considerable rationalization and improvement. The 1902 Education Act created local authorities and empowered them to coordinate elementary and secondary education. It allowed them to fund 'voluntary', that is church, schools, to the fury of the nonconformist population, who saw this as the government subsidizing sectarian Anglican or Roman Catholic education. Indeed, some very respectable citizens went to prison for withholding their rates on conscientious grounds. This measure was never rescinded even by the Liberal government of 1906, with its strong nonconformist flavour, and gradually it received reluctant acceptance. It was important to the two Moravian schools at Ockbrook that Derbyshire, along with other authorities, took seriously their involvement in secondary education. Secondary schools, which were fee-paying, appeared in Long Eaton, Ilkeston, Alfreton and Derby. The Liberal government then insisted that schools such as these should admit at least 25% of pupils from public elementary schools free of tuition charges. The Ockbrook schools were no longer relied on by the public so heavily in the exclusive provision of secondary education to local children.

Meanwhile, the Moravian Church worldwide was conscious that state involvement in education constituted a challenge. It was proud that there were 713 Moravian schools in 1911, which were intended to work towards the aims of the Church 'to evangelize the Nations and to educate Youth', in the words of Bishop M.W. Leibert, which were reported in the *Moravian Messenger* vol. XXI (15), 1911. While the Bishop declared that 'the Moravian Church is honourably discharging its full quota of obligation towards the enlightenment and uplift of humanity', he admitted:

> On many an old wall and in not a few bare rooms is written the verdict of our times, in a strong, bold hand, to the effect that well-nigh universally our equipment is both antiquated and inadequate.

Finance was a problem: Moravian schools depended on 'unreasonably low' fees, on variable support from congregations and the Church's provinces, and on capital, if any, which had been accumulated through occasional surpluses. Furthermore, while schools were well managed, teaching staff were not as well qualified as they might have been—not for lack of trying; indeed, their qualifications were improving, but so were those of teachers in state schools all over Europe. In Germany particularly Moravian schools were running very hard to stay in the same place—and were still losing the race. Teaching had always been seen as a form of 'ministry' in the Moravian Church, and teachers were not paid as full professionals. These worldwide issues may explain the difficulties which the Ockbrook schools experienced during and immediately after the First World War.

If the new headmistress of the Ladies' School, Miss Emma Elizabeth Titterington, had such problems, they were nothing compared with those of Mr Ernest Walder of the Boys' School—his school had to close. Numbers had dwindled, and expenses had become too great. In the summer of 1914 the Provincial Education Committee voted decisively to keep the School open, but within a month £3,000 of capital (an enormous sum in those days) had to be written off to clear debts. Accounts show that Ockbrook Boys' School was quite significantly more expensive to run than any other Moravian school open in England, costing nearly fifteen percent more per pupil to run than the Girls' School or than Fulneck Boys' School. The Committee's nerve failed them, and one member declared in debate: 'The day of private secondary education is done; - [such schools] can only compete with the endowed schools by violation or by neglect of hygiene laws.' By early 1915 the Boys' School had reached the end of the road, and a farewell meeting was held on 6 April, before the boys and staff were transferred to Fulneck. The Girls' School was by no means free of financial difficulties, but while the Church was subsidizing the School to some extent, it is obvious that the position was not serious enough to cause immediate closure.

It will be remembered that the girls were accommodated and taught in the three houses above the Church which they had occupied for a century, those known today as Liley House, Ivy House and Sisters' House. The closure of the boys' school was an ill wind which blew beneficially to the girls, as it meant that they could move into the building thus vacated, which—with much adaptation and extension—has been their home ever since. They moved immediately, at the beginning of the Summer Term of 1915, and Miss Titterington could then begin in earnest her work of developing the School and keeping it in line with both Moravian tradition and modern trends in education.

Miss Elizabeth Titterington

Elizabeth Titterington was 29 years old when she became head—the same age as Miss Harvey on appointment. She held an honours degree in History and an MA from Manchester University; she was an intellectual and—by the standards of her time—a feminist. She was committed to the life of the Moravian

Community. Her photographs show a tall and handsome woman, who must have lent distinction to public occasions and commanded respect. As we shall see, she made many educational and pastoral innovations in the twelve years before she married and left. First, let us complete the account of the School's financial tribulations.

The First World War was not a time of poverty and economic decline: in fact, real incomes increased during the conflict. The slump came in 1921. Yet the School was impoverished during the War. In 1918 the Church offered to transfer the School to the County Council, but the offer was refused. The Finance and General Purposes Sub-committee of the Derbyshire Education Committee, meeting on 31 December 1918, 'could not at present see any prospect of making use of the premises.' No reason is given in the minute of this meeting, but elsewhere it is suggested that the County saw no need for another grammar school so close to those at Ilkeston, Derby and Long Eaton. A similar solution to similar problems at the Moravian girls' school at Fairfield was in this case found to be possible: the Lancashire Education Committee adopted the school as Fairfield High School for Girls.

In 1915 there were only 24 pupils in the School; this rose steadily year by year to 78 (including 16 young boys) in 1919. There had been three staff when Miss Titterington was appointed in 1914; since one of these was a Froebel-trained junior teacher, it was scarcely enough for the modern secondary curriculum the new Head had in mind. By 1920 there were five full-time and three occasional teachers, and 93 pupils on the roll. HM Inspectors, however, reported that the Moravian Union was still subsidizing the School and was likely to continue to need to do so. After that, numbers dropped dramatically—to 53 in 1926—but the School was solvent by 1922, not requiring a subsidy. Day fees had been £7. 17s. 6d (£7.88 by modern reckoning) per annum for the youngest pupils and fifteen guineas (£15.75) for the over-fourteens in 1920, and were nine guineas (£9.45) for the juniors and eighteen guineas (£18.90) for the oldest girls in 1924.

The records we have do not offer any explanation for the sudden drop in numbers and the seemingly contradictory improvement in the School's finances. The economy of the nation suffered a setback in 1921, it is true. There is no suggestion of incompetence on the Head's part: inspectors praised Miss Titterington as an excellent head, and they deplored her and the other teachers' low salaries—as well as the low fees charged. Maybe she had inherited an impossible financial position, and certainly she had enabled the School to run more efficiently in the 1920s than it had earlier. It was an amazing achievement: even sixty pupils at an average of thirteen guineas produces only £819.00, from which a head and five full-time staff have to be paid and the School has to be maintained. Derbyshire County Council was paying its women teachers between £130 and £350 a year, depending on experience and qualifications, in 1919. Ockbrook staff (except the Head) were admitted to hold modest qualifications at the time, but even so, the figures are surprising.

LIFE at the School during the First World War was full of variety. The physical move into the former boys' school in 1915 was very entertaining for the girls. Lessons were clearly disrupted as they rushed from building to building with furniture and piles of books. In the now empty girls' school building, they gleefully rang the bells whenever they passed. To move a few yards down the street is in some ways no less trouble than a long-distance transfer. Much of the move was effected with the help of the porter's barrow, which was intended for transporting coal. The removal men were middle-aged, and one of them, in Miss Titterington's words, 'was so drunk that the foreman begged me to get rid of him, as he could not do so himself'. It all sounds great fun.

When war broke out, Ockbrook became host to the Fifth Northern General Hospital, and wounded soldiers occupied the Lecture Hall. The Commandant of the Hospital was Mabel Nelson, who figured briefly in Chapter 3, and whose name crops up again and again in its history as a pupil, teacher, friend and ally of the girls' school. Convalescent soldiers had used a sitting room at the back of the boys' school and continued to do so when the girls moved in; they were 'no trouble', according to Miss Low. Indeed, very good relations were established with the Hospital, and the Head and teachers occasionally took stints of evening duty to give the staff a break.

Elizabeth Titterington's innovations were many. In her very first term dramatic performances became a regular feature of the School's artistic life. It is hard for us at the end of the twentieth century to understand the sense of unease with which some church people contemplated the theatre in earlier days, but an extract from a minute of the Ockbrook Elders' Conference from 1871 explains the misgivings. The Provincial Elders had written of

> 'a growing tendency to introduce in the public recitations given by our schools the representation of scenes of a dramatic character, and we feel that it has now become our imperative duty to state our decided disapprobation of the practice and to urge that it be altogether abandoned. We deprecate it as being likely to produce in the minds of the young a fondness for theatrical exhibitions, which may be a snare to them in their future life, and a stumbling-block to others as being inconsistent with our Christian calling, which requires us to avoid the appearance of evil...'

The Ockbrook boys' school had once held such an entertainment before 1870. Permission for it had been sought from the elders by Mr Shawe, the Headmaster, but it had been agreed to 'reluctantly' and it had given offence to some members of the congregation. Theatrical presentations were not by any means unanimously

Wounded soldiers recover at Ockbrook, c. 1916

opposed, however, as the very fact that this matter surfaced demonstrates. As early as the 1840s a pupil at Wyke Moravian school reports her intense pleasure at having taken part in a performance of 'Masterman Ready', clearly an adaptation of Marryat's novel. In the second half of the nineteenth century dressing up and acting were very much part of Settlement life in Germany. Comenius himself had recommended 'enactment' as a means of perceiving the reality behind words. Perhaps Ockbrook was particularly puritanical in this respect; but by 1914 opposition was clearly much reduced, and Ockbrook girls have participated eagerly in theatrical presentations ever since, as a vast library of photographs in the School archives testifies.

The curriculum was reorganized to take into account the requirements of public examinations—the School Certificate, which until replaced by the General Certificate of Education (GCE) in the early 1950s was not a single-subject examination: it was necessary to pass at least one subject in each of five groups in order to obtain a certificate. It became usual for all girls to take this exam; no longer did the school advertise in the *Moravian Messenger* the successes of *individual* candidates. The Head was not able immediately to provide for good teaching of all subjects, and mathematics and science were recognized as a particular

The gymnasium in 1920

weakness. Nevertheless, in 1920 the School was 'recognized as efficient' by the Derbyshire Board of Education, and thus achieved national acceptance as an independent school.

Miss Harvey had introduced sport; Miss Titterington made physical training compulsory. Hockey and netball were the winter sports, tennis and badminton the summer games. Gymnastics entered the curriculum and became popular. The girls played tennis on the club courts in Borrowash until the School built its own in 1926.

As a vehicle for friendly competition in sport, the house system was introduced in 1917. Great figures from Moravian history were chosen for the names, and they survive to this day: John Amos Comenius, the great pioneer of modern education, Wenzel von Budowa, Czech soldier-hero from the sixteenth and seventeenth centuries, and John Cennick, the eighteenth-century poet and evangelist. In 1922 Girl Guides and Brownies were instituted. In 1923 domestic science entered the curriculum.

Our knowledge of Ockbrook School in the second half of Miss Titterington's headship is greatly assisted by the *Ockbrook School Magazine* which was reinstituted with no. 13 in 1921, having been silent since no. 12 in December 1914, and by Miss Low's booklet; a dispassionate outsiders' view is given by the two HM Inspectors' reports held in the Public Record Office. Miss Titterington herself left a very brief account of her work, and at the time of her death many old girls and former colleagues sent in their memories of her to the School Magazine in 1957.

The Inspectors' first visit took place for one day only on 30 March 1920, and the overall result of it was that the School was 'recognized as efficient', a seal of approval by the State, but not one which gave any rights to receive funding from government or local sources.

The picture these reports give of the School is very clear. It was a very small school, strongly weighted towards the younger end: 31 of the 78 pupils in 1920 were under nine years old. There were only ten boarders. Thirty-four pupils were aged twelve and over. There were two girls studying for London matriculation exemption: they doubtless had higher education in mind. Two recent old girls were studying at Manchester University in 1920. A quarter of the pupils came from Ockbrook itself, half from the rest of Derbyshire and the remainder came from further away. The sociological composition of the intake consisted of 40 percent from professional families, 14 percent farming, 12 percent wholesale traders, five percent retail traders and contractors, 22 percent clerks and commercial agents and 7 percent public service. Eight pupils held scholarships or grants covering some of their tuition expenses. A quarter came from public elementary schools. The main career ambitions of the girls were to enter teaching or take up secretarial work.

The staff in 1919. On the front row are Miss Low (left), Miss Orr (with cat) and Miss Titterington (in gown)

The premises were described as 'pleasantly situated' and the classrooms and boarding accommodation 'well arranged'. The main defects were given as the cloakrooms for boys, the library provision, and the equipment in the science laboratory.

The curriculum consisted of Scripture, English language and literature, history, geography, French, Latin, mathematics, botany, nature study, hygiene (alternative with zoology), drawing, singing, physical exercises, handcraft and needlework. Piano, violin, dancing, gymnastics, swimming and cookery were available as 'extras'. The best-taught subjects were scripture and Latin, with English and history not far behind. The inspectors recommended that more time should be given to French, and they criticized quite strongly the teaching of mathematics and provision for science (which consisted entirely of the biological sciences).

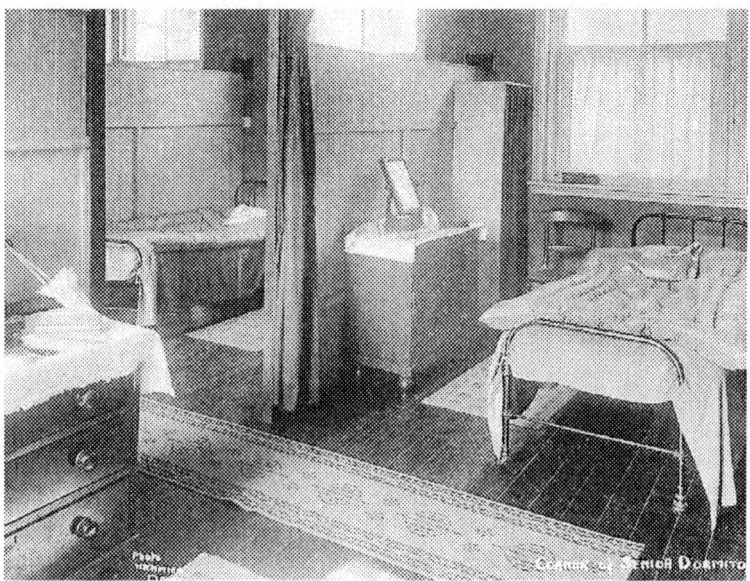

Four views of the School between the wars

1914-1945

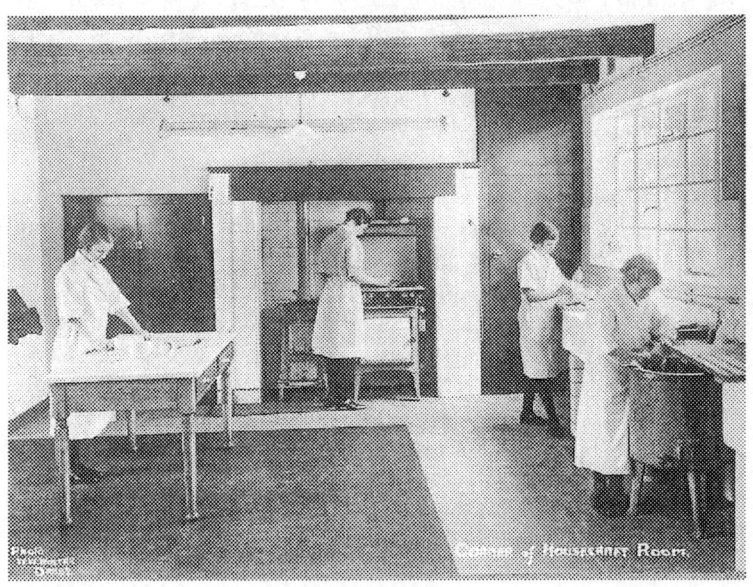

The staff were not all fully qualified—there is some contradiction in the inspectors' remarks here, since in one place they claim that there was only one qualified teacher, and in another they list both Miss Orr and Miss Low as fully qualified. Even so, the message was clear: Ockbrook must have well-trained and adequately paid staff, or it would not continue to make the grade.

The main strengths of the School appear to have been the 'energetic, capable and efficient' head, and the fact that 'the corporate life of the School is healthy and vigorous'. Moreover,

> The tone and discipline of the School are excellent, and it is evident from the frequent visits paid by former pupils that a warm bond of affection unites them to their old School.

The Inspectors came again, this time for two days, in 1924. They noted that the School had not been a charge on the general funds of the Moravian Church for the previous three years, but the numbers had declined and the general picture had changed quite radically. There were now only fifteen pupils under nine years of age, in place of 31. The boarders were up to 27 (almost treble the 1920 figure), but day pupils were down to 37 (from 65). The total was 64 (78 in 1920). Little real improvement in the premises, including the library, was seen, the head was still 'energetic and efficient', salaries were still very low, but science teaching—now in the hands of a newly qualified graduate with a teaching diploma—was much improved, despite this teacher's lack of experience.

Miss Titterington had clearly raised academic standards and ambitions amongst the girls, since several had done well at Higher School Certificate, and old girls were now studying at Manchester University and at the Reading and Nottingham University Colleges. One girl had won a County Major Scholarship in 1923, ninth in order of merit among the fifteen successful applicants. (Grants for students in higher education were very hard to come by at this time.) The inspectors mentioned on both occasions that the majority of girls stayed at school until the secondary course was completed. This was a 'performance indicator' of some importance in the early twentieth century, when parents still tended sometimes to remove their daughters when *they* felt they had had all the education a girl needed.

Reports of the content and quality of teaching are much more searching than in the 1920 inspection. The ground covered in some subjects was cause for some doubts: the variable syllabus in History, the exclusive concentration on staff notation in music, the limited time (still) devoted to French, the relatively uninspiring written work in the senior classes in English. These are to be set against promising innovation in mathematics and science, the 'very fair' standard in the junior classes, and 'creditable' teaching in many areas.

In the previous chapter we referred to *The Star*, the school magazine duplicated by 'jelly' which had been instituted by Mary Harvey in 1901. From 1909 to 1914 it was the *Ockbrook Girls' School Magazine*, and was properly printed with a photograph of the School on the front cover. It bore the legend 'New Series' from no. 5, for some reason, and these words survived on the title page until 1975 or later. In 1921 the journal was reinstated and became the handsomely produced and printed *Ockbrook School Magazine* (which we shall refer to henceforth as *OSM*). This journal tells us a great deal about the School in Miss Titterington's era. Her foreword to the first issue is witty and self-effacing: she herself was the only member of staff to sit on the editorial board, and the rest of the work was done by girls of all ages. The editor was Connie Winn (later Fawcett), who became a governor and served for many years in the 1960s, 70s and 80s. (By 1926 the editor was Elise Birtill, who was later to become Headmistress.) *OSM* contains many contributions of all sorts: creative writing, news of old girls, and a chronicle of school life.

The 1921 issue refers to the foundation of an Old Girls Association—another of Miss Titterington's imaginative innovations. From this time on, regular news of old girls helps us to construct a picture of the service the School was performing to society in general—more will be said of this later. There are accounts of visits to the School by people distinguished in their field, reports of excursions and educational trips, attendance at theatres, concerts and lectures outside the school, articles and reviews of dramatic and musical performances, a school trip to Paris, and always a lively account of the literary society meetings. The new guide and brownie packs figured prominently. Examination successes and sports activities were, of course, reported regularly. For such a small school to be able to mount so much stimulating activity is a tribute to its staff, and in particular to Miss Titterington, who insisted upon raising the level of intellectual life among the girls.

Among the visitors was the composer and musicologist Geoffrey Shaw, who came to lecture on hymn tunes. An interesting sequel to the visit was that Dr Shaw, who, with his perhaps slightly better-known brother Martin, was an editor of *Songs of Praise*, named one of his hymn tunes 'Ockbrook' as a compliment to the School. It appeared as number 354 in the (undated) 1920s edition of the *Public School Hymn Book*. Unfortunately, the tune is set to words which are not really suitable for modern-day school worship: 'Not for our sins alone Thy mercy, Lord, we sue'. The metre too is slightly unusual, so other words which fit the tune are hard to find. In consequence 'Ockbrook' has fallen out of use.

A popular character at Ockbrook School from 1924 was a dog called Larry, which the Head adopted. Larry became the subject of many essays in the *OSM*, including a 'spoof' autobiography and an account of his journey to Ockbrook. In fact, when Miss Titterington married and left in 1926, her portrait appeared as frontispiece to the magazine, but Larry's constituted the endpaper. He was seen at her wedding wearing a school tie; he did not go to Scotland with the couple, but ended his days in Ockbrook with Miss Nelson.

A very significant mention of Miss Titterington in these magazines is:

> The Literary Society held a debate on March 24th [1922]. Miss Titterington moved that 'There should be equal business and professional opportunities for women as for men.' The motion was opposed by Marjorie Dinnis. Needless to say, the women had an easy victory!

We may find some irony in this brief item. Miss Titterington was unquestionably a gifted and able woman. She had reached a high status in her chosen profession of teaching. She could have continued, perhaps moved to a larger school with even more scope for her talents, and made a very distinguished career. But she gave it all up. Why? Because in 1926 that was what women did when they married. Only a decade earlier, women teachers working for the London County Council (and doubtless many others) had to agree 'not to keep company with young men'. Marriage and teaching were considered incompatible. So the 'business and professional opportunities', open to Miss Titterington, were closed to her as Mrs King.

Professor Leonard King held the Chair of Zoology at the West of Scotland Agricultural College, which was affiliated to Glasgow University. The couple therefore left England, but returned to live in Ockbrook in retirement. Mrs King regularly contributed essays and other items to the *OSM*, writing from Glasgow often under the pen-name of 'K'. She died in 1957, her husband a year later.

At the time of Mrs King's death, many Old Girls paid tributes to her in the *OSM*. Their personal memories refer to a wide range of characteristics: some remember her inspired history teaching, one remembers the way she introduced girls both to the classics of literature and to modern art and books. 'Her lessons on the Gospels must have influenced the lives of many of us,' writes a third. She had a sense of humour, and she was genial and kind, buoying up one recent old girl who was seriously ill with regular Mabel Lucy Atwell postcards; but at the same time she was a firm disciplinarian, believing in courtesy and good manners. A good conversationalist, the girls enjoyed their turn at sitting next to her at meals. Most significant of all, she raised academic standards without detracting from the moral and character-training aspects of education.

MISS Jessie Farquhar Orr had been Miss Titterington's deputy for eight years, and in 1926 she took over the headship, which she held for nineteen years. We have now reached the period in the School's history which many living old girls remember. The School was still small, though it was growing: by 1944 it reached a total of 133 including 47 boarders. Even this is very small by modern standards. Moreover, while six boys and twenty-four girls were admitted to the school in the year 1928/29, they were all of different ages—there was no really firm pattern: pupils came and went in a more haphazard fashion than is normal today. In 1929-30 there were only 34 girls of secondary age in the School, and 72 altogether. Numbers in the forms were Preparatory: 15, I: 8, II: 13, III: 12, IV: 16, V: 5 and VI: 3.

The HM Inspectors' report for 1930 gives a picture of the work of the School at the time. It had established 'a happy environment and a sound education'. Behaviour was good—it was 'a pleasant and friendly place'. The destinations of leavers included a small number going into higher education, while the majority went into 'commercial' work, and hospital or nursery nursing. In 1929 one had gone into poultry farming, and one into training for physical education. The mention of poultry farming recalls an anecdote from one old girl, who left in the 1930s after a very successful academic career at the School. Her younger sister, however, was not suited to the life of learning, and Miss Orr kindly and tactfully suggested: 'I think it would be a good idea if you took your sister with you when you leave. She'd be very good at looking after the chickens!'

The curriculum at this time consisted of scripture, English, history (and current affairs in form V), geography, Latin and French, mathematics and science. A more interesting and valuable scripture syllabus would have been taught, the inspectors believed, if only the School would drop its devotion to the Cambridge Junior examination (a pre-School Certificate exam of which the inspectors did not approve). Mathematics was good, geography involved 'work of real value'. The only science taught at this time was botany, but it was developing well. Latin and French were limited in quality and standard. There was some weakness. 'Miss ———'s knowledge is not equal to her enthusiasm...Her use of modern methods is characterised more by zeal than by discretion.' There were plenty of games, though gym was charged as an extra, 'surprisingly, and some girls do not take it.' The Library still needed an input of material if sixth-form work was to be developed. It is notable that Elise Birtill, one of the most distinguished pupils at the time and a future headmistress of the School, left Ockbrook after taking her Higher School Certificate to prepare for entrance to Oxford at a school in Bristol.

'Carriage and speech' were praised by the inspectors, as were the extra-curricular activities. Art, needlework and music lessons were not visited or commented upon.

As before, the staff (six full-time and three visiting) were held to be poorly paid and not very well qualified. The directing board (we cannot strictly speaking call them 'governors' in the modern sense) explained again that in the Moravian Church teaching was seen as a form of ministry and was not undertaken 'for commercial gain'. Miss Orr herself protested to the inspectors that the poorly-qualified staff she had at her disposal would 'hardly fare better elsewhere', and the inspectors admitted there was some truth in this remark. Tuition fees were still what they had been in 1924, from nine to eighteen guineas per annum; boarding and tuition £66. 3s plus laundry £1. 11. 6d. It had been necessary for the Moravian Church to make good some deficit in the School's finances around this time.

The School Magazine for the 1930s and 1940s gives a an impression of the School's work and activities, even in the wartime, of remarkable stability. Throughout this period, school sports—tennis, cricket, netball, hockey, swimming, and the athletic sports day are regularly reported. Ever so many plays were given throughout the period, even if in the early war years performances took place in daylight because of the blackout regulations. The Literary Society met regularly, and its meetings seemed to be of a great variety: poetry, debates, play-readings, and often dancing to close with. A rambling club at one stage replaced the literary society, but the rambles usually ended at some place of historic importance, such as Southwell Minster. The Brownie and Guide packs were intensely active. The Old Girls were welcomed to School annually. Pupils learning French attended French plays and during the war formed a French Society. At Easter 1939 Miss Orr had the courage *not* to cancel a trip to France, despite the threatening international situation. Miss Orr celebrated her birthday annually with a party for the senior girls. The girls made many visits to concerts, plays, recitals, and lectures outside school. The annual visits of a Mr Broadhead are reported year in, year out: he would give a recital (what today would be called a one-man show) in which literary extracts and sheer fun both figured. The variety of this activity for such a small school is remarkable. The only feature which some old girls from the period remember as tedious is the occurrence of lectures for the boarders on missionary activity in remote parts of the world. The school log-books do seem to show that these became rather over-frequent.

In relation to the excursions, a visit to Chester in 1928 was marked by a potentially disastrous incident. Miss Orr writes:

> As a party was about to set off up the river in a rowing boat, one girl trod on the side and tipped the whole party,

including the gym mistress, into the river. I can still see Lilian Webster standing dripping in front of me, saying, "Oh, Miss Orr, whatever shall we do?" We decided that they should go to the Turkish Baths to be dried and warmed, and when they joined us for tea at Bollard's no-one could believe they had been in the water, so spruce were they.

Evening prep ('probably with /Miss Low in charge', adds one old girl), 1931

Alison Robbins has contributed the following sketch of life at Ockbrook at this time:

From April 1935 to July 1944 I was a termly boarder. I was just six when I came, so my first term was spent in Lower Prep. with Miss Low. Miss Low had three classes in one room, Lower and Upper Preparatory and Form I. Teaching was strict and formal and we all sat in rows in our desks, forbidden to speak unless spoken to, or without first putting a hand up. This classroom was situated on the second floor.

Rules were strict: there was no talking or running in the corridors or on the stairs, and no running up or down the stairs two-at-a-time. Needless to say, we were sometimes caught sliding down the banisters. Such splendid banisters were irresistible. There were Order Marks for such misdemeanours.

During my first three years or so, our uniform was the traditional gym-tunic, with navy viyella blouses in winter, and white silk blouses in summer and for gym and games. Ties and girdles were red, but there were House Colours for special occasions. When summer dresses were introduced, we were very pleased. They were in a fine checked cotton material in red and white.

Outdoor uniform in winter included navy-blue greatcoats and black velour hats with red hat-bands. We had black woollen stockings too, which we also had to wear on Sundays in summer, with our white silk dresses with the big floppy black bows. The Sunday dress in winter was navy-blue, with a white collar. We had navy gabardine raincoats for general wear, red jelly-bag caps and red-white-and-blue scarves. On summer Sundays we wore white serge with panama hats and white gloves. We were expected to keep these white outfits clean: a tall order for young children.

Junior dormitory was on the top floor, a very large room. I do not remember how many beds there were, but probably about twenty. They were iron bedsteads with wire meshes on which the mattresses lay. There was an island of chests of drawers in the middle of the area, and we all had drawers with our names on. Senior dorm. was over the dining room.

For the youngest children the first rising-bell went at 6.45 a.m., and I remember having to strip to the waist and wash in a bathroom which had beautiful ferns of ice on the window-panes in winter. There was no hot water on tap in the mornings, so a huge zinc tub was carried up two flights of stairs by two maids, and we had to dip the hot water out of this and into a basin in order to wash. There was plenty of scalding hot water for our bath rotas in the evening.

When bells went for meals, we all had to line up in the corridor on the first floor, in silence of course, juniors on one side and seniors on the other, and proceed down to the dining-room in single file when the mistress on duty gave the order. Miss Orr herself stood at the head table to serve the midday meal, and we took it in turns to take the plates round. We were allowed to talk during meals, but if we became too noisy, we would be silenced for a few minutes, and then talking could be resumed quietly.

After the end of afternoon school, day-girls went home and we boarders went upstairs to change out of uniform and into our own dresses. There were no jeans or slacks then. We did our prep in Miss Low's room, between tea and supper, and then we were free to play. There was a playroom for Juniors, a sitting-room for Seniors and a third room for prefects and sixth-formers. Prep had to be handed in the next morning, and there were shelves outside the staff-room door for this purpose. We all had positions in class according to our marks of the previous term, and there were prizes and certificates on Speech Day at the end of the Summer Term. A mark of 75% or more earned a First Class Certificate, 65% a Second class. There were medals also for sport, swimming, music, etc., and other prizes (books) for things such as gardening. I have three or four of those. Anyone who was interested could have a small patch of ground in the vegetable garden, usually shared between two, where we could grow marigolds, pansies, lupins and such, as a hobby.

There were exams at the end of every term, and Cambridge School Certificate and Higher School Certificate for VA and the sixth form. Some girls went on to university, but there was very little formal discussion of careers. There was no biology or science really, though we did have botany. Miss Orr considered that the Arts were most suitable for girls, so I left at fifteen, with my School Certificate and Matriculation exemption, to study natural sciences. I was never in the sixth form.

Gardening as a hobby, introduced as we have seen by Miss Harvey, was clearly still enjoyed. The encouragement of good school examination results by the award of certificates indicates attention to high standards of attainment. Miss Orr's reported attitude—which would today be considered highly old-fashioned—

that the arts were more 'suitable' for girls may explain why the provision of science was so lacking until after the Second World War. Yet at the same time, and in fairness to Miss Orr, we should note that just before her retirement a science laboratory was installed in the school, and that she herself declared: 'For long it had been a crying need.'

Another Old Girl (1934-38), Muriel Hassall, née Bestwick, adds to Miss Robbins's information that on Speech Day the girls wore white silk dresses with a black bow tie. She recalls a number of the mistresses of the time: Miss Christine Andrews, the deputy head—'rather glamorous for Ockbrook', Miss Blue (shorthand and typing), Miss Emery (games), Miss Wood (music)—who 'wore her hair plaited into earphones!'—and her namesake Miss Margaret Wood (geography). The redoubtable Miss Low 'always had an order mark on the end of her pencil'. She it was who taught botany in the upper school as well as taking charge of the primary classes. Mrs Hassall later served as a Governor for about twenty years.

During Miss Orr's headship the premises were modernized and improved in various ways. A gymnasium was built in 1930; the swimming bath was improved and heating for it installed. A new floor was laid and many enjoyable dances held there. In 1931 a new reference library was opened; to encourage its use general knowledge competitions were inaugurated. At the same time electric light and the telephone were installed. Then a stage was installed in the dining hall, ending the tiresome necessity of erecting one every time one of the numerous plays was given.

Miss Low recounts the story of how the primitive bathing arrangements were improved:

> Until Miss Orr became Head, all water used in any part of the building had to be pumped, a great deal of it by hand. There was a noisy engine that pumped water for the radiators, but that was all. Water for the baths...had to be pumped by hand by the mistress on duty; one had to pump a hundred times to get a really good bath...In addition to pumping the mistress stoked the bath furnace every fifteen minutes, so she was kept busy...
>
> I well remember one day at the end of the holidays...when Mr Batt and another of the school governors walked in to look around. He asked me how the baths

were filled and I began to pump. Then I suggested that he might like to have a go. He began, and after a minute dropped the handle, remarking as he did so, 'This is no job for a woman.' By the autumn term the baths were moved...and connected to the heating arrangements—and the mistress on duty ceased to pump!

Miss Orr adds that the removal of the baths allowed that part of the building to be dismantled and tennis and netball courts set up. 'Some regret was felt when the baths departed from what was...called the pump room, for it was a great treat after your bath, to get a friend to bring your supper, and then you could make French toast in front of a roaring fire.'

Next, the old kitchen, unused since the days of the Boys' School, was remodelled into a domestic science room. The old hockey field on Bakehouse Lane had reached the end of its useful life, and the present sports field was bought, levelled and drained, and used for the first time for sports day in 1938. A science laboratory was opened around 1945.

THE SECOND World War had a profound effect on the whole of national life. As throughout its history, Ockbrook School had welcomed overseas pupils and staff; in the 1930s there had been pupils from the Netherlands, France, Germany and Switzerland, and the War disrupted such friendships. In the early months, until the invasion of France, far more British civilians were killed in this conflict, by aerial bombing, than combatants. Derby, with its Rolls-Royce works, was a prime target for enemy bombers, and we now know from the memoirs of wartime scientists that the beams used to guide the Luftwaffe to their targets were being bent to mislead the pilots, often re-directing them in their ignorance as far as Nottingham. Ockbrook often had enemy planes overhead; as everywhere else, no gleam of light was allowed to show through the blinds to offer the aircraft any tempting target. 'What a time we had painting every window with anti-shatter liquid, and later covering them with muslin!' wrote Miss Orr.

The air-raid sirens sounded frequently, and there were many disturbed nights. Soon it was decided to move the desks upstairs and the beds down, so that the air-raid shelter could be reached by everybody with relative ease. Conditions were very crowded, and Miss Low reports having to sleep for a week in a bed infested with plaster and rubbish after a ceiling had come down on top of her. She does not attribute this accident to vibrations from the extremely noisy naval gun, which was placed in the fields behind the School, near Dale Road. The little boys in the junior department enjoyed collecting shrapnel from the tennis court on their way into school after a raid, and she would make them turn out their pockets, since many of them would otherwise have scarcely been able to sit down. Two staff were required for fire-watching duties every night, and quickly learned to find their way around outside in the pitch darkness.

Wartime drama in daylight. A Midsummer Night's Dream, *1942*

An elementary school was evacuated to Ockbrook for about a year in the early part of the War, and two of the teachers lived at Ockbrook School; the teachers used Miss Low's living room occasionally for staff meetings. When Derby School was evacuated to Ashover, about five boys who had been Ockbrook pupils returned to the School temporarily. Domestic help was difficult to obtain and the girls sometimes had to help with routine cleaning and cooking. Rationing and food shortages were a major problem, though Miss Orr is reported to have been an excellent manager in the kitchen. In one of her wartime speech-day reports she proudly declares that no-one has gone hungry. Miss Low writes: 'We had a wonderful variety in our meals. Of course, some people grumbled—they always do.'

Miss Low's evocative account of an Ockbrook night on duty during the War is well worth quoting in full:

> One night, typical of many, I lay, of course, partly dressed, on the bed in the dark and gloomy tunnel, at the end of which a tiny lamp threw weird shadows on the walls and ceiling. Suddenly the comparative silence was shattered by a scream. What was it? Do I rush to find out? No, it was only someone calling from the Land of Dreams. Silence now, soon broken by sounds of snoring from further parts of the building—easily heard, as everyone slept with open doors—the creaking of a bed and the sound of stealthy footsteps as someone wakes up and decides to wander in search of water or a change of scene. Again a period of silence, broken once more by cheerful sounds of quiet laughter and merry voices slightly hushed. What now, I wondered, surely not a party? No, only the usual pleasantries in fifth-form dormitory. Quiet once more, and then a gentle sound that comes down the wooden stairs. What now? Only Smoky, our pet grey kitten in search of a wandering mouse. Silence again, broken by bangs and sounds of tramping feet—surely a bomb has fallen somewhere near! No, only some of the staff retiring for the night after working late, and shutting the staffroom door. Thus the night passes to the accompaniment of other 'noises off', and I doze with one ear open and hope that nothing dreadful will happen. Hours pass, and again sounds are heard like a distant train drawing nearer. What this time? Only the maids, those early risers armed with brooms and buckets. A distant bell rings loudly and sleepers begin to stir. Matron comes along to every room with a cheerful 'Good morning!' I spring out of bed and rush off to prepare for another day.

The School Magazine for the war years reflects the situation: poems referring to Hitler, Churchill and air raids. There were waste paper collections for the war effort, and successful National Savings drives. Savings may not seem to us today to be a very exciting topic, but it was the School's success in this field which reached the news columns of the *Derby Evening Telegraph* in 1941, taken from Miss Orr's Speech Day address. News was published of Old Girls, mistresses and former mistresses who were in all parts of the world and in all branches of the women's armed services. International travel was dangerous and unpredictable: one person reported on a 'wonderful' sea journey from Australia (with four U-boat warnings), while some pupils did not return to school from Ireland because of the danger. At the same time, marriages were reported between soldiers, sailors and airmen and Old Girls and young mistresses. This led to a new feature of life at Ockbrook: when Miss Dora Blue married RAF Sergeant Condy on 1 November 1939, she returned to her work at the School, probably the first married woman to teach there full time. The next year, Miss Andrews (not the former Deputy Head, who left in 1936) married a young man expecting call-up, and returned to the School as Mrs Lawley.

Miss J.F. Orr

Miss Orr inspired great affection in her pupils, who mentioned her dignified, but not pompous manner, her striking appearance and pleasant smile (but she did not often smile, apparently), and the way she brought special qualities to the three roles of teacher, headmistress and guide captain. One former pupil wrote when she died in 1957: 'I appreciated her kindness and endless patience, and in bringing up my own children I have so many times thought about her and tried to follow the example she set me.' Miss Orr remained in Ockbrook and taught French and Latin in her home for many years after her retirement in 1945.

During Miss Orr's tenure of the headship there was an increasing awareness of the important roles women could play in society. This was stimulated by the War, but not exclusively so. Mrs King, the former Head, gave away the prizes at Speech Day in 1939 and reminded the girls of the importance of qualifying 'for something, and [that they should] not leave school without some definite ideas as to how we were going to make the best use of the years ahead.' A few years earlier Miss Orr had urged girls to stay on longer at school and become better trained. A Speech day guest in 1934 who stressed the moral aims of education, rather exaggerating the unimportance of examination success, was even subtly contradicted by Miss Orr. In her time academic standards were maintained and improved, music and the arts flourished, the all-round development of young people was richly fostered through sporting, intellectual and cultural activities, and by the end of the War the School was full to overflowing with pupils. A foundation had been laid for the major expansion of the School in the post-war years.

Chapter 5

PROGRESS AND EXPANSION. 1945-1974

THE SECOND World War ended in Europe in May 1945 and in the Far East in August. All at Ockbrook enjoyed the public holidays which celebrated victory in Europe. There was at the time a distinct feeling that a new world was dawning, though many of the hopes of the peoples of the world for peace and freedom were soon to be dashed. Miss Orr took the opportunity to bow out, having presided over nineteen years of successful expansion and growing achievement, while maintaining a 'spirit of service and duty' at the forefront of school work, as was said in a tribute to her at her last speech day. The School chalked up one hundred percent success in School Certificate in 1945; four fifths of the candidates achieved matriculation exemption. She handed over to a distinguished Old Girl, Elise Birtill, who was to lead the School for twenty-five years.

Miss Elise Birtill

Miss Birtill was 34 years old at the time of her appointment. There had been Birtills in Ockbrook since the eighteenth century and one of them had been in charge of Ockbrook Ladies' School briefly in the 1830s. Elise Birtill was a pupil at Ockbrook from 1921 to 1927; after studying for Oxford entry elsewhere, she went to Somerville College and gained a first-class degree in Modern Languages. She taught at two well-known girls' schools: Withington High, Manchester, and Putney High School. When the London school was evacuated to Bath during the War, she taught French at Bath High School.

In mid-1945 there were 146 pupils including 45 boarders, and by the following year this had grown to 176, including 50 boarders. There were eleven full-time staff. Throughout this history we have noted fairly wide fluctuations in the numbers of pupils, but these figures after 1945 represent the fact that Ockbrook was reaching what one might term a critical mass. There is a point at which a school is much better able to cater for the efficient teaching by specialists of all subjects in a modern curriculum: in a small school the teachers have to double up on subjects taught, and when one leaves, she is usually harder to replace than a single subject specialist. This difficulty may lead to over-reliance on part-time teachers. Ockbrook was becoming much more obviously a school for academically-minded girls; Miss Birtill, as we shall see, set out to develop the sixth form and to consolidate this reputation for excellent results. Places were being offered to girls from the local education authority.

Money was a particularly difficult problem in 1945-46. It was a time when the *Guardian* reported, in view of a 'tough' government policy towards independent schools, that *all* such schools were having to increase their fees 'drastically'. The Burnham scale for teachers' salaries was becoming universal, and Ockbrook was having to raise its staff salaries to reach the national norms. (Ockbrook's fees were among the very lowest in the country.) At the same time national insurance and pension contributions were introduced. Meanwhile the local governors protested at the low pension offered to Miss Orr. There was a hefty deficit of a thousand pounds in the School finances in 1945-46. For many years the School lived from hand to mouth: Miss Birtill would write to the Governors for 'five hundred pounds because the current account is depleted.' In one case she offered to take a cut in her own salary to finance the appointment of a new teacher. In 1946 tuition fees were only five to ten pounds a term, but by 1953 they had reached twelve to eighteen pounds per term, depending on age.

An Old Girl, Ann Hall Pollack (now retired in Colorado), gives a first-hand impression of the School as Miss Orr handed over to Miss Birtill.

1945-1974

The tone of the School in 1944-45 reflected the emotions of the country on the brink of peace. Miss Orr ruled over a school which was a tranquil refuge from wartime for so many of us. Nevertheless, it hardly escaped. Fathers and brothers were killed or taken prisoner, mothers often were doing full-time war work. There must have been girls who lost their homes in the bombings. Ockbrook residents opened their doors and their hearts to refugees and evacuees. Quite a few of us took Red Cross first aid courses at the home of Mrs Addy. We gave concerts to raise money for the Red Cross. We endured constant bomb drills. We sometimes shared airgrams from our fighting relatives. Often, we shared special gastronomic treats. We joined the Brownies and the Girl Guides, and even played cricket (made more attractive by the sight of Miss Boyd's brother egging us on from a distance), until enthusiasm waned somewhat when our First Eleven was roundly beaten by the Second Eleven at Nottingham High School for Boys.

Form 5A, in which I was one of fifteen girls, did not escape the wartime scars, and I can recall several whose fathers were killed or taken prisoner by the Germans or the Japanese. My own father was a gunner on merchant ships and my mother worked for the BBC in London, which was, I was certain, a prime target for German planes and flying bombs. Add to this wartime scenario the rising hormone level of fifteen to seventeen-year-olds combined, of course, with the absence of male influences and the prospect of the great unknown—peace—and you had a dynamite mixture in the fifth forms in 1944-45.

The girls of 5A were very creative. They were quick to sense the insecurities of others and, having exhausted those of their peers, turned upon the teachers. Miss Lois Parish, who taught English literature and history, was a prime target. Miss Parish was petite in stature with reddish hair drawn back in a bun, reminiscent of a Brontë or a Jane Austen. She was shy and blushed easily, which made her the perfect target for the emerging 5A bully crowd. The fact that she was a wonderful teacher who could bring a reading so totally alive that one really wanted to work on it did not discourage the girls. There was one memorable class when a 'spirit séance' was planned, using the library books covering the wall behind the teacher's desk and blackboard. Very strong, but invisible threads were attached to single books (Miss Parish was somewhat short-sighted) and, during the classwork, they would be pulled miraculously from the shelf by designated girls in the front row. After several books were thus deposited on the floor, Miss Parish sensed that something was not right. Terribly wrong, in fact. Exasperated, she blushed a shocking pink and rushed from the room. The curious thing is that there was not a girl, then or since, I suspect, who would not admit that their love for literature stemmed directly from Miss Parish, who, after her retirement, spent a lot of time corresponding with her old students.

When Miss Orr retired, her transition was made real to us, perhaps, only by the appearance of the slim brunette with a gentle manner who was to take her place. Miss Birtill was our new French mistress. We knew that she was also the new Headmistress. We sensed her insecurities as a new arrival—and appreciated her tendency to blush, and blush easily. We behaved badly. I can't remember quite what we did, but we probably only did it once. We had neglected to look closely at Miss Birtill's eyes. Kindly and observant when not challenged, they hardened considerably when angered and the blush that spread upward was a warning—not a show of weakness. I recall we tried 'the treatment' not more than twice after that. Miss Birtill had full control and the antics of 5A rather petered out from lack of success!

We may add that Miss Parish wrote a brief memoir of her career, 'Thirty years at Ockbrook', for the *OSM* no. 68, 1968-69, pp. 6-8, and that there is an excellent photograph of her in the same issue.

In 1946 Greenside House was taken over and a kindergarten started there. Sometimes senior girls helped in Greenside as part of their social training and perhaps as a taster for entering the teaching profession later. The gymnasium was freshly equipped; the science laboratory, planned in Miss Orr's time, was opened at a cost of £1,965 19s., and at last science lessons became an established part of the curriculum from 1946. The kindergarten was expanding, and the School offered the local church five shillings a week to rent the lecture hall: there was no deal, as the Church wanted a pound. Therefore in 1948 the Moravian Church on behalf of the Governors bought the Mount for £4,570 in order to accommodate the junior forms, and in 1953 both Broadstairs and the Grange unexpectedly became available for purchase: the School was not slow to buy both for £900 and £7,500 respectively. The three properties represented a substantial increase in the School's premises. In the early 1950s plans were afoot to extend the existing hall (the present dining hall), which eventually became a multi-purpose assembly hall, gymnasium and dining room.

A Parents' Association was started in 1946, and from October 1944 a group of locally-appointed governors had been assisting the Church board in governing the School. Previously, the School had been governed by three 'directors' from the British Province of the Moravian Church, but as the War ended and the School was expanding it became clear that a local board of advisory governors was needed in order to keep more closely in touch with events. While Ockbrook had been the headquarters of the Church, from 1825-75, this was no problem, but the mid-twentieth century required more systematic governance to be in place.

The School still managed to run its wide range of extra-curricular activities. Magazines for 1945 and 1946 refer to the Literary

Little Women, *1945*

Society, various talks, films, visits to theatres to see both English and French plays, art exhibitions and concerts, a newly-formed orchestra and choir, Mr Broadhead's annual recital, the guides, tennis, netball, gymnastics, swimming, hockey and cricket. The intended autumn 1945 production of *Little Women* was a success, except that it had to be postponed till February because of an outbreak of mumps. Miss Birtill herself was sometimes the choir director, though the main work was done (later in two choirs, junior and senior) by Miss Brewster, who taught at Ockbrook until 1950. It is interesting to read in the *OSM* for 1945-1950 of the growth of interest in co-operative music-making (as opposed to instrumental exams) and the progress of these musical groups. At first the orchestra's rendering of Haydn 'bears very little resemblance to the original', as one of its members reported in the Magazine, and success in competitive musical festivals was limited, yet by 1949 the senior choir had won a madrigal prize at Derby.

Sports Day 1945 was as much fun as ever. The spirit of the occasion is caught in these extracts from an article in the *OSM* entitled 'Sports Day 1945—and other years':

> The school is in utter confusion. Madly, girls run hither and thither, half dressed, hastily copying out programmes, changing, looking for lost articles of clothing. Mistresses forget to rebuke girls for running in the corridors. They run themselves. ...Presently a bell clangs harshly.
>
> Miss Boyd, with the megaphone, rushes up and down, hurrying us into position. Usually people either shiver in the wind or swelter in the sun and drink gallons of lemonade. Hearty people drink lemonade in any case. This year, however, the climate was temperate.
>
> In the races, each girl struggles hard for her house and cheers lustily...There was even a race for the mistresses this year, and another for the parents. Everybody laughed, but nobody minded.
>
> After the races, we all go back to school. The girls go to the grass tennis courts to have a bun and lemonade. Lucky ones have two or even three buns.
>
> After that we go into the gym to hear the results of the races. Parents have by this time wandered into the hall. They clap now and then, when they think about it. Then

they have to listen to a few short speeches, after which they wend their way homewards, consoling themselves with the thought that next year it may rain.

The remaining boarders persuade Miss Bayne into giving them some tea, which they badly need.

Cynthia Ridgway

Competitors on Sports Day in 1947

The School Magazine published a few comments from new girls who arrived at the school in the late 1940s. Their comparisons were, for the most part, unflattering to the schools they came from. They liked the red uniform, the rural setting, the 'good lighting and heating'. They were impressed by the variety of activities, and although they were kept very busy and had more prep than in some other schools, they also thought they had more free time. Busy, interested and free, therefore; moreover, they asserted 'the staff take an interest in the girls.'

Nothing could be clearer than that Miss Elise Birtill set out, as we should say today, to raise the profile of Ockbrook School, and to ensure that it remained a force to be reckoned with. She was a woman of strong personality, successful experience as a classroom teacher in other schools, and high academic qualifications. Moreover, she had a philosophy of education which she sought to disseminate through 'Headmistress's letters' in the *OSM*, directed at Old Girls, parents and—most of all—present pupils in the School. In her letter for 1947, for example, she invited old girls to offer their 'maturer reflections' on their schooldays. She quotes one who had written: 'My debt is almost unrepayable to Miss Orr and her staff, who gave me something nobody could ever destroy or take away—a fine education'. It is easily to 'sentimentalise over the past,' writes Miss Birtill, '...but we must see that our ideals are kept fresh and our work continually creative.'

In this same article Miss Birtill reveals her desire to strengthen sixth-form studies at Ockbrook. In the 1940s the great national increase in education for older teenagers had barely begun. The school-leaving age had only just been raised to fifteen by the 1944 Education Act. Some future undergraduates went to university with School Certificate 'Matric' though usually 'Higher' qualifications were needed. Post-sixteen classes were small. Miss Birtill admitted that the Ockbrook sixth form was rather too small to grant the best advantage to the girls concerned. Quoting Dame Dorothy Brock, however, she asserted that the influence of a sixth form on the School was more significant than might at first appear. Given a sixth form,

> The whole school catches a different standard. Side by side with the advanced work of the few goes the culture of the many...To preserve scholarship for the few is to enrich the many.

These concerns are reflected in the report of HM Inspectors of Schools, who visited Ockbrook from 11 to 13 October 1950. This was the first time the school had been inspected since 1930, and it had changed quite a lot since then. There were now 219 girls, including 67 boarders; 87 (including 12 boys) of primary and 132 of secondary age. Some of the secondary pupils were paid for by the Derbyshire County Council. Most of the leavers went in for some form of further or higher education: in five years 22 had entered secretarial training, 8 nursing, 6 universities and 8 non-university teacher training, while others had gone in for housecraft, agriculture, art, music or librarianship. There were ten regular and seven visiting staff.

The most severe criticisms were levelled at the premises and domestic arrangements: the dormitories were rather cramped, the kitchen far too small and the meals unbalanced and not nutritious enough, the gym was too small, there was no hall, the classrooms were over-full, the reference library poorly stocked, and more play space was needed. Miss Birtill made good use of these criticisms to strengthen her arm in arguing for new buildings and for adaptation of the existing ones. The Governors were aware of the problems, and, as we have seen, acted when space became available.

The Inspectors had confidence in the Head and the Governors, and stated that the qualifications of the staff, while not exactly outstanding ('with one exception'—it must have been Miss Birtill herself!), had greatly improved since 1930. The Head was underpaid and overworked and should have secretarial assistance, they said. (Most of her letters to the Chairman of Governors in the archives are in longhand.) It was a school of 'steady, honest endeavour' rather than brilliance, and it is not hard to see that the Inspectors felt the girls would benefit from more challenge in nearly every subject in the curriculum. Miss Birtill herself weighed in in the School Magazine, reminding the pupils that they had a responsibility too:

> I am beginning to wonder whether some of you are not suffering from the fear of being hardworked rather than the actual reality? With a sense of purpose and a courageous effort to overcome difficulties much more could be achieved and less would be heard about not having time for this or that subject. How quickly the demon of self-pity can undermine the will to work is a fact which gravely disturbs me, and I hope you will fight it vigorously whenever you recognise it in yourself.

What the Head had realised, but many girls and even teachers had not, was that from 1951 they were in a new educational environment. When School Certificate and Higher School Certificate were replaced by the General Certificate of Education Ordinary and Advanced levels, it was not merely a question of renaming the old exam. 'School Cert' had been a group examination in which all subjects had to be 'passed' for a certificate to be granted. The GCE O level was a single-subject examination in which as many certificates were granted as *subjects* had been passed. A good deal of twaddle was talked at the time about falling standards: 'You can now get a School Cert by passing only one subject.' Well, that was in a way true, but it missed the point completely. A pass in one subject only was very little use to anyone, and, moreover, the new pass level had been raised to that of the old 'credit'. It was intended that pupils who wanted to continue the study of subjects to A level would by-pass O level and not take the exams for these subjects. This idea was very soon discarded; it fell victim to the English mania for collecting bits of paper which are believed to represent academic achievement in themselves.

The implication of the inspectors' remarks is that staff were tending to teach to the old pass level as if it still existed, without stimulating pupils to raise their sights. Even if standards were raised, everyone needed to look beyond and strive for broader aims and a wider general culture. It was a question of responding to a world in which educational prowess was to be more important than ever before, and where a nominal level of achievement was simply not going to be sufficient.

Elements of the School which earned high praise from the Inspectorate included the music teaching (though many instruments were in a poor state and a better gramophone was needed), and the standard of spoken English in all subjects in and out of class. 'The appearance, general demeanour and, in particular, the natural and interesting conversation of the girls made a very favourable impression. They were delightful to meet and it seemed clear that they grow in character and personality as they pass up the School.'

The School was, therefore, morally in a good state, but Miss Birtill and the Governors had to develop the premises considerably, and improve the quality of the academic education offered. The Head made no exaggerated claims for the Inspectors' report, declaring it to be 'satisfactory'—as it was—and rolling up her sleeves to get on with the work of improvement, 'underpaid and overworked' as *she* was. 'This is certainly no time to indulge in complacency about past and present achievements, and it is vital that the School should continue to grow—not necessarily in numbers, but in the scope of its work and activities as well as in buildings,' she wrote in *OSM*. This is precisely the response which was needed.

1945-1974

THE TONE of Elise Birtill's headship—high academic standards, hard work, attention to a variety of worthwhile activities, belief in what is nowadays sometimes rather deprecatingly termed 'high' culture, responsibility to the wider community, all with an eye to the future development of the School, for the benefit of all pupils, and its ability to respond to contemporary requirements—was now set. The ensuing twenty years of her tenure of office were a period in which Ockbrook continued to develop. Buildings continued to be acquired, adapted or built. In the 1950s permission for building had to be sought—not from the town and country planners, as they were then called, but from government itself, which was severely rationing building materials in the post-war race to build housing. 'We had hoped that by now [summer 1952] the proposed new hall would be in existence, but we were, alas! frustrated by the severe restrictions placed on all building operations this year. No amount of importunity has moved the powers that be,' wrote the Head. When this hall (the present dining hall) was eventually adapted, a room was set aside as a reference library and reading room and a building fund was announced to extend the library, which inspectors had been criticizing since 1920. A new sports field was inaugurated in 1954.

The 1960s were filled with fund-raising activity to provide for necessary further improvements to the School's premises. Unfortunately, the very success of the appeal which was inaugurated led to friction. The Appeal Committee came into dispute with the Governors as to the priorities in accordance with which the money should be spent. Lawyers were involved, and threats were made that all money subscribed would be returned to those who had given it. It seems that a relatively small group of parents was using 'underhand methods', as the Governors put it, to wrest the initiative from the Governors, who had final responsibility for the financial affairs of the School. This dispute was cautiously aired on speech day in 1962 in an attempt to defuse the situation. Whatever the turbulent Committee wanted, the Governors could not even if they had wished delegate their responsibility for the school's policy in this as in any other field.

By 1964 tempers had cooled, and a new wing was completed, containing a new classroom and specialist teaching space for biology and physics. It was opened by the Bishop of Derby. The domestic science room was extended by the generosity of an anonymous parent. The house north of the Church, which had previously belonged to the School, was re-acquired in the same year and used to house the weekly boarders. It was felt appropriate that it should bear the name of Lydia Liley, the day school principal who took over the Ladies' Boarding School in the 1870s, but in fact it had been occupied by Lileys long before Sister Lydia's day: a Rev. and Mrs Liley lived there in the 1820s. The building appeal fund grew steadily through the 1960s, and finally on 28 November 1967 the 'Birtill' Hall, as it is known today, was informally opened; an official opening was performed by the Duke of Devonshire on 11 May 1968. Another guest of the School (he opened the fête in 1967) was the popular folk singer, Cy Grant, who had become a national figure through his appearances on the extremely successful daily television programme 'Tonight'.

Academically the School made steady improvements during this period. The relatively small numbers of girls in the sixth form mean that sometimes there were quiet years, sometimes with no university entrants. Of course, at this time a very small proportion of the population attended university: five or six percent. Yet in 1954 three Ockbrook girls were successful in getting into Oxford, and this at a time when women's colleges were few in number and a phenomenally high standard for entry was required. The new GCE O level examinations were regularly entered by twenty to thirty girls, and A levels attracted seven to twelve candidates in these decades. In 1954 there were twenty girls in the sixth form, which the Head regarded as a milestone.

The wide variety of activity sought by Miss Birtill is reflected in reports in the School Magazine. School plays, *Twelfth Night* and *Androcles and the Lion*, to mention only two, sometimes gave way to opera and operetta: *Dido and Aeneas* in 1953 and *HMS Pinafore* in 1963. Drama emerged in the early fifties as a school subject, and the drama classes often gave performances when no formal school play was mounted. 'Drama' then was not quite the subject it is now, with extemporization and creative exploration of situations of various types, but would more correctly be termed 'theatre'. One governor of the time reports that his attempts to ensure that the new Birtill Hall was a flexible space for modern drama teaching were frustrated by the majority, who wanted—and got—a stage with curtains and 'none of your nonsense with girls rolling around the floor and expressing themselves'!

1945-1974

The Head started a philosophy group to discuss the world of thought. There was a debating society in operation for most of the time—the 'art of argument' was not allowed to fall into disuse—a Local History Club, a Science Society, Arts Society, Geographical and Travel Club, and the Student Christian Movement. There were many visits, outward bound courses and youth hostelling weekends. Sport was, as ever, popular at Ockbrook: hockey, tennis, swimming, athletics and gymnastics were engaged in with the greatest enthusiasm and house and outside matches were keenly contested.

The pupils were skilled at raising money. Efforts for the building fund did not displace collections for a wide variety of charities such as Oxfam, refugee relief, the PDSA, for Christian Missions and for the restoration of the local church cupola and its organ.

Christingle services were instituted in 1953. It is perhaps surprising that this feature of Moravian Church worship was not a regular aspect previously. Part of the School's service was broadcast by the BBC in 1961. More than one local church of other denominations has instituted Christingle services as a result of attending them at Ockbrook.

Music was strong in the School at this time, and many girls entered for graded examinations. The orchestra was revived in 1955 after a brief period in abeyance. Operas, as already mentioned, were occasionally performed. A music club was started in 1958, for the purpose of inviting first-class professional musicians to give public recitals. Between 1958 and 1964 well-known artists who appeared included Florence Hooton (cello), Kendall Taylor (piano), Gerald Moore (accompanist and lecturer), Professor Ivor Keys (piano), Thea King (clarinet), Evelyn Rothwell (Lady Barbirolli, oboe), Celia Arieli (piano) and the group Intimate Opera, which was led by the pianist and famous 'talker about music' on the radio Anthony Hopkins. A relatively large membership of pupils, parents and local people was needed to make this Club viable, and when membership fell below the necessary one hundred and artists' fees increased, the society was disbanded in 1965.

Ockbrook School received many visitors from abroad as student teachers and pupils: their native lands included Denmark, France, Belgium, Germany and Czechoslovakia. Photographs and magazines show that there were African or Caribbean pupils

Tennis players, 1946

at Ockbrook as early as the late 1940s, when Britain was far from the multi-racial country it is today.

The changing atmosphere as regards the role of young women in society was reflected by a number of things at this time. We recall that in the early 1920s the girls of Ockbrook voted by a large majority that the same career opportunities should be open to women as to men. In 1962 Sir Robert Robinson, 'one of the greatest living scientists', was the guest of honour at speech day. He said:

> It would be strange indeed if I were not an enthusiastic supporter of scientific careers for women. Not only did I enjoy the collaboration in research of my late wife over a period of more than forty years, but I have had the opportunity to meet women chemists of all ages...It is really forcing an open door to argue the value to the nation, nay even to mankind, of the actual and potential contributions of women scientists...
>
> It is therefore essential to provide the school laboratories in which the girls can receive the elementary training which will enable them to develop their aptitude in the future...I warmly approve of the ambition of Miss Birtill to make Ockbrook into such a school.

1945-1974

The message was reinforced the following year at speech day by Dame Janet Vaughan, Principal of Somerville College, Oxford, who 'spoke of the wonderful opportunities awaiting adventurous girls who are determined to succeed...She recalled how she herself was told when young that she would never make a doctor, but she...became a leading research scientist in the field of medicine.' Dame Janet and Sir Robert must have been pleased to learn that the Scientific Society at Ockbrook had 80 members.

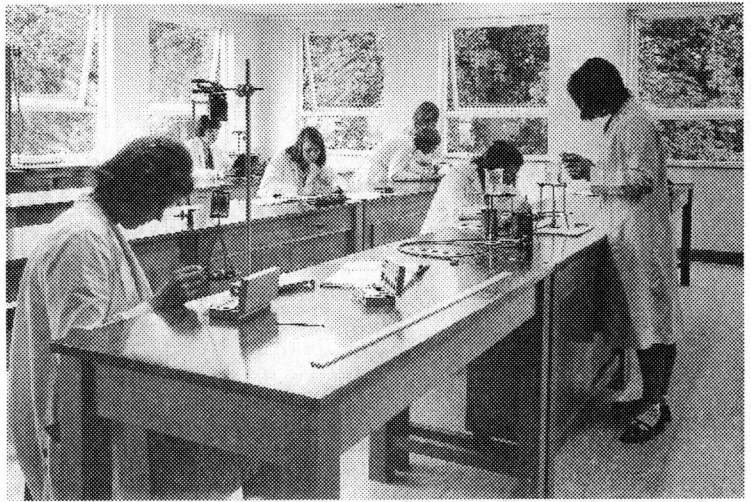

Physics laboratory, 1960s

The year 1968 was marked throughout the world with unrest of all sorts. Events in Czechoslovakia, when the Czechs attempted to introduce 'Communism with a human face', were parallelled by student unrest in France and Germany and a 'long, hot summer' in the USA. British educational institutions had their 'time of troubles' too, but we have no record of any occupation of the office at Ockbrook or a sit-down protest in Settlement Road. One girl wrote in the School Magazine an eloquent defence of protest songs as a genre of popular music and social concern. But perhaps the most interesting response to a changing cultural world is a few remarks by Lois Parish, the lady whose teaching abilities were so warmly commended in Mrs Pollack's reminiscence above, who taught at Ockbrook for thirty years and who retired in 1968. It shows that the best teachers never close their minds to new ideas and trends, and can learn from their pupils:

> During thirty years I have seen certain changes of taste in reading, some of them understandable, though a little hard to accept at the time...A marked feature of recent years has been a decided preference for the direct, stark and even crude: 'penny-plain' in fact, rather than for the magical lines of the Romantic Age 'twopence-coloured'. This taste shows itself in hair-style, dress, and daily life as well as in literature. Whether it is permanent or transitory, who can tell? Much of the new writing I have come to appreciate with the help of my pupils and my younger colleagues, so that, although not always a patient Griselda I could emulate her creator, the clerk of Oxford 'And gladly wolde he lerne and gladly teche.'

Miss Lois Parish

Miss Parish's concern for education survived her: she left money in her will to endow sixth-form scholarships at the school she had served for so long.

What was everyday life like at Ockbrook in Miss Birtill's time? It must have been very busy, and while girls were urged by the indefatigable Head to keep their noses to the grindstone, the many sports, cultural events and activities must surely have prevented boredom or idleness ever getting a toe-hold. Pupils visiting from abroad throw light on the atmosphere of the School. Two German girls in 1961 found this English boarding school 'new and exciting'. The 'rhythm of the day' encouraged every opportunity for understanding between pupils and teachers, as they were in such close contact. The Germans were impressed by the cooperation between parents and staff, and they reflected that the day girls formed the connection with the larger community. Dutch girls the following year were struck by the wearing of uniforms, the playing of outdoor games in winter and the wearing of gowns by the staff. They found the boarding-school fare rather hard to learn to like: Yorkshire pudding presented particular difficulty. It was very clear none the less that Ockbrook School had 'a very happy atmosphere'. Tributes in the magazines to long-serving members of staff indicate that Ockbrook had a high degree of stability without suffering from hardening of the arteries: many part-time and temporary staff came and went, while Miss Parish completed her thirty years, Miss Harris twenty-seven and Miss Low a full fifty. Another member of staff, Mrs Pilling (formerly Miss Boyd) completed over thirty years in 1972.

Miss Birtill was unconventional and informal in some ways: one new resident teacher describes arriving on appointment and being shown a completely empty flat. 'Never mind,' said the head. 'You and I will go shopping for furniture and curtains tomorrow.' She inspired great loyalty and affection, while being tough in ridding the School of troublesome elements. But when she retired there would be no more weekend marmalade-making in the boarding house. No longer would the Head press-gang the staff into making raffia mats round the supper table in aid of the Spring Fair!

Fees at the end of Miss Birtill's headship were between £20 and £48 for the Junior Department and £62 per term for the Seniors. Full boarders paid £75 per term and weekly boarders £68. Materials for needlework and art were charged extra, as were textbooks and musical instrument tuition. Games were charged five shillings (25 pence) a term and boarders had to pay five shillings for the use of 'wireless, television, record players and newspapers.'

When Miss Birtill retired in 1970, she left a school of 331 pupils, far more than she had ever expected. She had taken the job in the first instance for five years—which extended to twenty-five. She left an establishment with greatly extended buildings, and with better facilities, though there was a long way to go before they would match the new curricula for the modern world; standards of academic achievement were more in line with the new demands of contemporary society and they allowed pupils to take their places in society as modern young women. Moreover, Miss Birtill attached the greatest importance to character building in the spirit of Christian teaching, and never lost sight of this ideal. She was greatly respected in the Moravian

Church, and was unanimously elected to the ancient office of *Advocatus Unitatis Fratrum in Anglia*, which carried with it a seat at Synod. The person elected to this office should be someone whose presence would not only 'add lustre to the Synod, but whose knowledge, aptitude and dedication to the service of God and through God to Mankind would be of great benefit to the Church.' Elise Birtill died on 16 February 1981 and is buried at Ockbrook.

Miss Birtill's successor was The Rev. Dr Arthur James Lewis. The appointment of a man to head a girls' school, though not unique, was in 1970 very unusual indeed, and the Governors felt it necessary to write to the parents and justify the step:

> Although this appointment represents a break with tradition we are confident that, given the full cooperation of parents and staff, Dr Lewis will serve the School with distinction and maintain the high standards which it has always sought to achieve.

Dr A. J. Lewis

Dr Lewis was appointed by the Provincial Board of the Moravian Church after two rounds of interviews. He was a Moravian, an educator of considerable experience in both secondary and higher education, a poet and hymn-writer, a scholar in the field of doctrinal theology, a fine preacher and speaker on public occasions, humorous, affable, friendly and hospitable. He was aged 56 on appointment. He had studied philosophy and literature for his first degree and had taken an MA at Bristol University; he had been a master and headmaster at Fulneck Boys' School, Principal of Fairfield, the Moravian theological college in Manchester, a lecturer in the theological faculty at Manchester University, and a senior lecturer at Newton Park teacher training college in Bath. He had spent half his career in the ministry as a regular pastor in churches, and at the time of his appointment to Ockbrook was minister at Higher Openshaw, Manchester.

'Brother Jim' Lewis, as a Moravian minister, had a high sense of loyalty to the Church, and he believed that he should fulfil his vocation as and where the elders of the Church decreed. After this very varied previous career, Ockbrook constituted a new, doubtless stimulating, and perhaps unexpected challenge. When he arrived, he took over Liley House as the Head's residence. It had previously been used for the weekly boarders.

When the new Head took over, examination success was at a high level: in 1970 there were thirteen entrants to universities and polytechnics and six to colleges of education from the sixth form. Tennis, netball, hockey, gymnastics and swimming continued to flourish; so did the Guides and a variety of other school activities. School plays in the early 1970s included *The Importance of Being Earnest*, *As You Like It* and *The School for Scandal*. In addition to these productions there were opportunities for Ockbrook girls to take female parts in school plays at Trent College (then a boys' school). At this time there were many joint activities with Trent and Repton: dances, dancing lessons, debates, play-readings, performances of 'Messiah'. The feasibility of holding more joint events was discussed. Not all these occasions were a success: one play-reading was 'badly organized' and 'rather pointless', and a joint school dance on one occasion appears to have been a fiasco. Nevertheless, the vast majority of co-operative ventures were beneficial to pupils of all the schools concerned.

Ockbrook mounted a performance of Coleridge-Taylor's 'Hiawatha' in 1974, and in the same year the very first dance display was given, to the great interest and enjoyment of all. A joint debate was held at Fulneck, and the Head Girl remarked that the art of debate had not been practised at Ockbrook for some years—yet the girls were able to put on a creditable performance.

The school magazines contain a good deal about careers advice, which Ockbrook had been taking seriously for years. There is reference to experimentation with different forms of worship in assemblies at this time. In 1973 both Christingle services were recorded by BBC Radio Derby and the senior service was broadcast on 26 December. A junior drama festival of one-act plays was held. Outings were frequent: to the Derbyshire dales and Bradgate Park, to theatres and concerts at Derby, London, Nottingham and Stratford. The School celebrated its one hundred and seventy-fifth anniversary in 1974, when the fête was opened by the television personality Michael Aspel. Dr Lewis entertained prefects and senior staff to dinner at the Post House, and on at least one occasion they cooked a co-operative meal at the Lewises' house.

Prospectuses of the earlier part of Miss Birtill's period had announced that 'all the usual' subjects were taught: this was at a time when there was no national curriculum, and when questions might arise as to what *were* the usual subjects in the science or languages curriculum, among other matters. However, by the 1960s and 1970s they are listed:

English Language and Literature, Religious Knowledge, History, Geography, French, Latin, German, Mathematics, Biology, Physics, Chemistry, Music and Class Singing, Art, Domestic Science, Dancing, Gymnastics, Swimming, and Games (Hockey and Netball in winter, Rounders, Athletics and Tennis in summer).

A regrettable but necessary change in the mid-1970s concerned scholarships and grants. Local education authorities were not able or willing any more to support pupils at independent schools, as they once had. Pressure on the existing trust funds increased in consequence. It remained possible, fortunately, for the Governors to reduce fees in case of hardship and to make some scholarships available. Nevertheless, in consequence of these changes in the willingness of public bodies to contribute to independent education, Ockbrook School was financially somewhat less robust in Dr Lewis's and Miss Driver's periods of office.

The School still had a substantial number of boarders at this period: its highest point was reached in 1966 with 114. There were between 90 and 100 in the early 1970s. Boarders were not allowed to be away from school except at half term, and they were permitted to go out only once (twice for the sixth form) in each half term on a Saturday or Sunday. Permission for outings was sought from parents, and the Head had to be approached in writing.

Dr Lewis did not remain long at Ockbrook, and so the experiment of appointing a man to a girls' school was short lived. After a bout of illness, Dr Lewis left in 1974. He took over a Moravian flock at Gracehill in Ireland. He expressed delight to be presiding over a church congregation again. When he left, the School was still strong in numbers: there were 344 in 1975. Even if, as the School Magazine said in its tribute to Dr Lewis—with its tongue in its cheek—'we were too much for him', he was remembered for his presence on public occasions, his dignity without false solemnity, and his sense of humour which 'expressed kindliness without sentimentality'. Dr Lewis died on 20 June 1990.

AS A footnote to this chapter it is instructive to look at the careers for which Ockbrook School was preparing young women between 1945 and 1974. No exhaustive list is available, but the *OSM* printed news of old girls in many of its issues. In those scanned we discover news of 308 mainly fairly recent former pupils. Of these 30 were at university or had just graduated, 53 were in school teaching and 11 in nursery nursing or working as a nanny. There were five doctors or medical researchers, no fewer than 62 in nursing or midwifery, and many others in medically-related jobs or training: physiotherapy 7, occupational therapy 7, radiology 9, speech therapy 3, pharmacists 4, one hospital almoner, one health visitor, one child care officer, one medical administrator, and there was one pathology technician. Secretarial, clerical or administration work counted for 34; there were 7 librarians, and one journalist. Ten went into agriculture and 17 into domestic science and catering. Three entered the armed services. Four were in banking or insurance, one ran a family business, 2 were in personnel work, 5 in management or public relations. Two were in scientific research and one a nuclear physicist.

There were 2 textile designers, 2 hairdressers or beauty-care workers, 2 in art or design, 1 in musical training, and 1 in social administration. Apart from three old girls in unspecified training, the following jobs (or training for jobs) were represented by one former pupil each: milliner, air hostess, university lecturer, telephonist, groom at a stables, cosmetics technologist, civil servant, dental hygienist, university administrator, and animal technician.

This list does not, of course, tell us how long the young women concerned stuck to their careers and how successful they were. The figures do not show the grade of the post occupied: for example, the pharmacists include one student beginner and one head pharmacist at a hospital, and the category 'agriculture' includes someone helping on the family farm and others in high-level training. We do know, however, that many of these old girls came to have distinguished careers in different fields.

The emphasis on medicine, nursing, medical-related and caring professions generally is very marked. Teaching and child care are also prominent. The other traditional female profession, secretarial work, is also strongly represented. While there are no engineers here, scientific research and business and commerce are beginning to appear. It is perhaps surprising that there is only one civil servant. Despite Miss Titterington's conviction as long ago as the 1920s that women should have the same career opportunities as men, and despite Miss Birtill's encouragement of scientific studies in Ockbrook School, the 'glass barrier' was not yet being dramatically breached. Yet at the same time Ockbrook girls were beginning to infiltrate some traditionally male professions.

Chapter 6

INTO THE MODERN AGE. 1974-1999

IN 1974 education in England was undergoing significant changes. Since the 1944 Education Act secondary schools had been organized according to the ability of the pupils, with the most able attending selective grammar schools and the less able secondary modern schools. In some areas technical or 'middle' schools were available to girls and boys in between these two categories. Independent schools like Ockbrook often took children who had passed the 'eleven-plus' examination, and who were paid for by the local authority, which was in effect buying grammar school places for some of its children in independent schools. When central and local government would no longer agree to this, the consequent loss of pupils affected the School adversely.

The system could not continue. The inflexible application of selection procedures at age eleven condemned some able children who for one reason or another had 'failed' this examination to what was regarded as an inferior type of education. Moreover, the percentage of pupils who were allowed into the grammar schools varied dramatically from eleven in some counties to thirty-five in others. Who would argue that children in Northumberland were three times less able than those in Manchester? The very idea was ridiculous, and this alone brought the selection system into disrepute. In any case, parents were not going to vote for a political party which advocated a system which might disadvantage their children.

Socialist principles were held by many teachers, and whereas in the 1940s and 1950s this meant *meritocratic* views—all who could pass, whatever their social background should be able to go to a grammar or independent school even if the state had to pay (and pay it often did on a sliding scale if the parents were not wealthy), by 1960 the comprehensive principle was gaining acceptance. Young teachers in particular often wished to teach in comprehensive schools, and there was a tide of opinion against selection, 'privilege', fee-paying and differentiation between pupils. Ockbrook was affected, directly and indirectly, by this wind of change.

The system was changing in other ways. While in the 1950s only six percent of school leavers attended university, in the following decade the numbers increased considerably. The Labour government headed by Harold Wilson had promised new universities, and many Colleges of Advanced Technology were awarded university charters. The polytechnics emerged as a significant force in higher education. As state schools provided opportunities to their pupils to enter such establishments, so did Ockbrook expand its pre-higher-education provision. While Ockbrook had the buildings, thanks to Miss Birtill's prudent purchases and extensions, new equipment and the constant upgrading of what the School had was necessary. Computers were not yet *de rigueur*, but the audio-visual revolution, which would have delighted the heart of Comenius, was well into its stride.

The new Head of Ockbrook, Miss Ann Beryl Driver, was a graduate of the University of Leeds, and had been deputy head of a school at Brighouse before coming to Ockbrook. She was a committed and loyal Moravian. She was a phenomenally hard worker, and needed to be, as she was faced with formidable tasks. She did as much as anyone to modernize the school. Changes in government policy throughout her term of office meant that she and the School—and all other schools—were living in 'interesting times'. By the mid-1980s momentous moves were taking place under the Conservative government towards a new Education Act which was to include a national curriculum. The introduction of GCSE, the General Certificate of Secondary Education, was another event which every school had to cope with, a radical change in educational policy and to some extent in attitudes. New books and a new, higher, standard of provision of materials were essential. The new head gave considerable attention to bringing Ockbrook up to modern standards of provision.

In the 1970s and 1980s Miss Driver gave further attention to buildings as well as equipment. Swallow's Rest was established as a centre for sixth-formers. Provision for art and craft was made by converting an old stable block; this was named the Mallalieu Centre, after the family which had built the large house nearby. Other troublesome matters used up quantities of administrative and emotional energy. The Birtill Hall was found not to be wearing well—suing an architect who had been dead for five years was no easy task, but it was done successfully and the building was rectified. Another supposed construction problem proved, after investigation by the University of Nottingham Department of Engineering, to be entirely imaginary.

Miss Driver and television star Christopher Neame at the 1975 School fête

Life at Ockbrook School was packed with action, as ever. Sports were as popular as they had been since they were instituted. In the year 1974/75 visits and excursions to the law courts, the Roman Wall, Dovedale, Coventry, Newark Show, Ironbridge and the All-England tennis championships at Wimbledon were organized. The choir sang, and it joined with Trent College or Repton for the formal performance of choral works. The orchestra was re-started. Junior drama festivals of short plays took place. A dance group won a competition in Derby. Eleven girls were confirmed in the Anglican or Moravian churches. There were debates, a mock election, a current affairs conference, an inter-house quiz, an exhibition of needlework to commemorate the achievements of the Sisters of long ago at Ockbrook. A television actor, Christopher Neame, famous at the time for his work in the 'Colditz' and 'Edward VII' series, opened the fête. Charity was not forgotten: there were collections and events in aid of Christian Aid and the Honduras floods. In the same and succeeding years there were bonfire parties; Miss Driver continued Dr Lewis's custom of inviting senior girls to a meal, and the candlelit suppers went on being held, with certain improvements suggested by Miss Driver. Professor Ted Wragg, who has since become an influential and popular figure in education, was the guest of honour at speech day; the Head Girl commented drily in the Diary that it was 'very humorous, for a change'. Social service as an activity was introduced by Miss Driver: senior girls helped regularly at a youth club for educationally sub-normal boys, and senior citizens from the Settlement were invited to tea.

During the 1970s and 1980s a number of musical works were performed jointly with Repton, then a boys' school: *Beethoven's Mass in C* and Verdi's *Requiem* among them. Two Ockbrook choir members, Iona Lewis and Caroline Sears reported their experience in the School magazine for 1977/78. Their piece conveys the fun as well as the educational value of the occasion:

> Pupils from IVB upwards started to learn Verdi's 'Requiem' for a performance in March. Progress was a bit slow because of the fact that we considered Latin a dead language and thought it should stay that way. However, we soon got used to reading the Latin and the music from the rigorous training we received from Mrs Heathcote, accompanied by Mrs Horobin substituting for a full orchestra on the piano.
>
> We practised every Monday lunchtime in the new Hall, not bothering when we got the odd bout of indigestion from hurrying our meal. When nature uncurled from hibernation (and there were better things to do) practices were increased to Thursdays as well as Mondays. Also, we were moved to the Church, where sub-zero temperatures lowered our morale considerably. A month before the final performance, we had visits from Mr Michael Salter (Christian name first discovered by courtesy of VB music O level spy ring). Mr Salter is the Musical Director from

Repton School. One of his visits was in the evening, when Mrs Heathcote brought members of the Sitwell Singers to aid and abet us. This was our first encounter with the tenors and basses.

Things really speeded up at Mr Salter's rehearsals; maybe this was because he had a rather loud voice and possibly because we realised that the performance was close at hand. We had two practices at Repton. When all performers were present the amount of noise that could be made greatly astounded us.

On the day of the performance we journeyed to Repton by coach. We practised with full orchestra and various other choirs for two hours, and afterwards we retired into the boarding houses for a good tea. When we had finished tea we amused ourselves by going for walks, playing games and listening to the radio. At a quarter past seven all the choristers met, loaded with Mentho-Lyptus, in the Library, which is adjacent to Pear's Hall, where the performance was due to take place.

Finally at half past seven we all filed into the hall where more than two hundred people were assembled to hear the choir and orchestra, who together numbered more than 250. The Choir consisted of singers from Ockbrook, Repton, Chesterfield, and even from as far afield as London. The orchestra was also very strong; it contained one particular percussionist who almost deafened those of us on one side of the front row.

The performance went very well and it was most rewarding to hear so much applause afterwards. We were congratulated by the Headmaster of Repton, Mrs Heathcote, Mr Salter, the soloists and members of the audience.

At about ten o'clock we all started to make our way home, greatly pleased with ourselves and perhaps a little saddened that it was all over. Later at School we pleaded with Mrs Heathcote to ask Mr Salter if we could participate in a further joint production and to our great pleasure we have been asked back to sing in another concert.

Miss Driver was responsible for other institutions which are now so much part of school life that one forgets there had to be a first time. On 8 October 1977 the first school Open Day was held. the Head Girl at the time, Susan Gillberry, reported in the school magazine:

> In the week leading up to 8 October School was filled with more bustle than usual. Staff were erecting elaborate displays, pupils were busy tidying up the building and hiding blemishes, and it was arranged that a number of girls should come into school on the Saturday morning. What was the reason for all this feverish activity? Ockbrook School was about to hold its first Open Day, to give parents and prospective parents an opportunity to look around the School and see a sample of pupils' work.
>
> Naturally every member of staff wanted to present her (or his) subject in the best possible light, and some had much greater scope than others to present their subjects attractively.

Mrs Kingsbury put up a large Art display and a Needlework display was arranged very hurriedly by Mrs Marshall in the temporary absence of a needlework teacher. In the Cookery kitchen a selection of dishes prepared by the girls was on show. They looked delicious, but it was probably just as well that visitors were not invited to sample them!

The Science staff had plenty to offer. the Biology Laboratory was filled with brightly coloured specimens: twigs and leaves, lots of rather nasty-looking fungus, tortoises and various other animals. The Physics laboratory was filled with various pieces of equipment and several pupils were on hand to demonstrate experiments to interested and somewhat amused fathers, who feigned ignorance, but who were probably Rolls-Royce engineers! In the Chemistry Laboratory Mr Hawkins set up several complicated experiments, using as much apparatus and as many brightly-coloured chemicals as possible.

There were History, Geography, English and Music displays. The French and German rooms were livened up with the use of tape recordings of music and conversation. One or two members of staff had much greater difficulty in presenting their subjects attractively. How on earth can one make Latin or Mathematics look interesting to the uninitiated?

The Library and the School Bookshop were both open, the latter doing a roaring trade, and there was a PE display in the Hall. The Mount was also open. School was open from 9.30 until noon, the aim being to show visitors the variety of courses offered in School and to show them examples of the work done by girls in each form.

By ten o'clock about three visitors had arrived and we thought that hardly anyone was going to come. However, we were soon proved wrong as they came in their droves and so many people enjoyed themselves so much that they stayed until well after 'closing time'.

In 1979 it was decided to institute a School Council. The Head Girl's Diary contains the following entries:

March 5th. There was a form period this morning for forms to discuss the school council. After a lot of dis-cussion over the past term it was decided that we should have a school council so that forms could bring up ideas and suggestions that perhaps they would not otherwise voice. This morning the representatives to sit on the council were chosen. There is to be eighteen members on the council; one repre-sentative from each form, two from 6B, one from 6A and the two head girls, two members of staff and Miss Driver. One member from 6B is also to be the secretary and the day head girl is to be chairman (so that's me! [Sally Hitchin]). Everyone has a vote, except for Miss Driver and myself but if needs be I have the casting vote. Since Miss Driver has to carry the can for anything, she can say 'No' even if the council decides 'Yes'.

March 12th. The school council had its first meeting after school in the library. Anne [Gillberry - the boarders' head girl] and I spent the afternoon rearranging the library furniture so that it looked like a board room (well, nearly). We also had chairs near the door so that people could come and watch, and quite a lot did. It all proved to be quite interesting in one way and another and most people were prepared to talk about what they had proposed. The suggestion of having a tuck shop was discussed, having more trips and discos and maybe a committee to organize them. The idea of having a quiet room for day girls to do homework was crushed for the very obvious reason that *home*work should be done at home. The idea of having better toilet paper was favoured but since a lot more would be used as tissues that one may not happen. There were a lot more things on the agenda but they will be discussed at the next meeting on 30th April.

The girls seem from this to have complied rather readily. Clearly the novelty of having a discussion at all was the prime ingredient of the meeting.

There were a number of issues in the early 1980s which required skilful handling. The School had difficulty in appointing and keeping good boarding staff. Girl boarders were demanding more freedom. The boarding house became a centre of interest for local youths. Miss Driver, for lack of support staff, was sometimes left in sole charge of the boarders. Often there was no-one to delegate authority to. Finance was part of the problem: the School's fees were relatively low compared with other schools, and when a surplus was achieved it was used to maintain the fabric. In view of the burdens which were ever increasing, it was proposed that Miss Driver should be encouraged to take a sabbatical term to recover her energy, but illness overcame her.

When Miss Driver fell seriously ill in January 1986, the duties of Head fell upon Mrs Norah Byron, who had only just succeeded to the post of Deputy Head the term previously. Mrs Byron, a former teacher at Loreto School in Nottingham, had studied Classics, but she was an enthusiast for her second subject, English. She had recently gained a Master of Education degree at the University of Nottingham. She had also contributed to that University's project on 'The Effective Use of Reading', which was highly respected among educators throughout and beyond the English-speaking world. In 1980 she had helped out at Ockbrook briefly during a maternity leave; she joined the full-time staff in 1981 as Head of English.

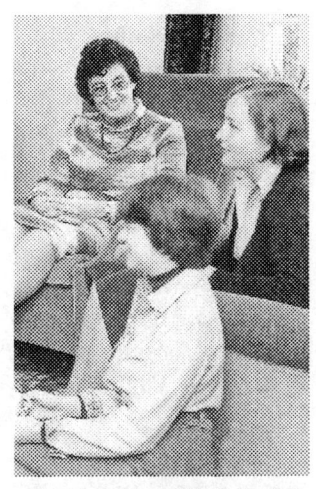

Miss Beryl Driver with senior girls

Mrs Byron was a Roman Catholic, and was therefore the first non-Moravian to act as Head of Ockbrook School. She served until Dr Myra Rennie took over at Easter 1987, when Mrs Byron returned to her former duties as Deputy Head. It cannot have been easy for her to hold the fort in these circumstances: Miss Driver had become very ill quite suddenly and a controlled hand-over was scarcely possible. Nevertheless, Ockbrook did continue to run smoothly; academic work, activities and sports went on as usual. There were changes and developments among the senior staff: Mrs Anne Beardsley took over the junior department, Mrs White was deputy head (boarding) and Miss Westland and Mrs Logie acted as deputy heads in staff, discipline and pastoral matters.

The new GCSE created considerable demands for teaching materials and the in-service training of staff. Mrs Byron's first priority was to see that the School was on a reasonably stable financial basis and in good shape when the new Head arrived at Easter 1987. At this stage Mrs Byron reverted to the role of Deputy Head, and worked happily with her successor for a number of years.

Dr Myra Rennie

When Dr Myra Rennie became Head of Ockbrook School she was in her early fifties, a research chemist originally from Edinburgh University, with school teaching experience at Christ's Hospital Girls' School at Hertford and St Albans High School. As Scots, she and her husband were Presbyterians—or, more exactly, members of the United Reformed Church, so Dr Rennie was the first permanent head of Ockbrook School who was not a Moravian on appointment, and the first married woman to hold the post. She soon joined the Moravian Church, there being no theological issue of great moment between Presbyterianism and Moravianism which could be seen as an obstacle.

Throughout the twentieth century Ockbrook, in common with all other schools, was continually obliged to adapt and conform to new initiatives and the requirements of government and society. We saw, in 1915, how the Moravian Church faltered and some declared that private schools could not possibly meet all the new demands placed on schools. These people turned out to be wrong, of course, but the need in all schools for new buildings, new equipment and new approaches to curricula, assessment, counselling, staff development and teaching methods never abated. Dr Rennie commented that on her arrival aspects of the school were in need of development, which is another illustration of the fact that at this period of educational change the whole national education service, including Ockbrook, was having to run very fast to stay in the same place. Her arrival coincided with the introduction of the new GCSE, and all that it meant. After centuries during which British governments had refused to become involved with school curricula, suddenly Parliament imposed a 'National Curriculum' upon England and Wales, something quite unheard of; indeed, government denied until the eleventh hour that it had an intention to impose any such thing. The National Curriculum did not apply to independent schools, or rather the law did not require them to adopt it. This merely created a further problem—if an independent establishment such as Ockbrook did not observe it, the school would be out of step with the whole national education system. The only solution was to sail along close to the National Curriculum, while not, perhaps, conforming to it rigidly.

Against this background, the findings of a review visit by the Independent Schools Joint Council highlight the factors which the new Head was already tackling. The 'visitors', or inspectors, were greatly impressed by the pleasant and orderly atmosphere of the school, and by the very good extra-curricular provision. Examination results around this time were variable, but at best quite excellent. Teaching was in many ways found to be very good indeed. There were still deficiencies in the provision of modern facilities, despite everything that Miss Driver and her predecessors had done to modernize Ockbrook. On the curricular front liaison with the junior department at the Mount needed to be strengthened, sixth-form general studies required revision, the visitors argued for a marking policy for the whole school, they said more should be done about drama across the curriculum, and that there should be greater curricular incentives for girls to stay on in the sixth form.

While the Governors had spent tens of thousands of pounds on the premises, the fitting out of rooms and laboratories for the teaching of all subjects was said to need modernization; computers were to be updated and made more widely available; more technical assistance should be available. At least, with a chemist as head, the science lab was fully equipped!

Dr Rennie set about her task with Scottish grit and determination. Staff appraisal—a matter absolutely essential in the modern age, whatever one thinks of it—was planned for. Development planning began. In-service training and the updating of professional skills were more strongly encouraged. More money was spent on books, materials and equipment. Buildings were made to conform with modern fire regulations. Labs and rooms were modernized. A computer room was instituted (there were only three computers, elderly BBCs, when Dr Rennie arrived), new classrooms took the place of some of the boarding accommodation which was no longer needed. A substantial extension and refurbishment of the primary department at the Mount was carried out. When more pupils under the recently appointed head of department, Mrs Beardsley, were recruited, they found very suitable accommodation there. The swimming pool was refurbished, but a much desired sports hall was considered, and at this stage found to be beyond the School's means. Dr Rennie made a sound financial policy a high priority—modern schools like Ockbrook simply cannot exist from hand to mouth.

1974-1999

Other matters reflect changes in society affecting Ockbrook. One issue of interest concerns the education of boys. Ockbrook is a girls' school, of course, but one which had traditionally admitted small boys to its junior department since the early twentieth century. The Sex Discrimination Act (1975) allows a school predominantly for girls to admit boys to certain sections or departments. In the early 1990s there was demand from parents that boys should be allowed to stay at Ockbrook until the age of eleven, instead of eight as formerly. This was agreed by the Governors, and is the present situation.

We saw at the very beginning of our history that Ockbrook Ladies' School was intended primarily as a *boarding* school, even though it opened with five day girls and only one boarder. The highest number of boarders ever achieved was 114 in 1966. Suitable staff was, as we have seen, difficult to recruit; Miss Driver had to 'sleep in' on a number of occasions in the absence of resident staff, while Dr Rennie escaped this necessity—narrowly sometimes. By the beginning of the 1990s boarding numbers were falling. Parents serving in the armed forces were no longer offered quite such advantageous assistance with educational fees

for their children as they once had been. In 1999 only about twenty girls board out of nearly five hundred pupils. The ethos of the age is against sending children away to school, but some parents, because of their professional situation or family circumstances, need boarding provision for their daughters, and Ockbrook has supplied a need here, though admittedly in recent years a small one.

Morning assembly in the Church, 1980s

One consequence of the falling-off in boarding numbers was that the relationship between the School and the Ockbrook Moravian Church changed. In the great days of boarding it must have been splendid for the local Moravians to have a strong body of girls in church on a Sunday morning. With a large day school, however, the presence of the School more often meant traffic jams in Settlement Road. Relations with the church remained good. Dr Rennie writes: 'We always considered it a privilege to use the church each morning for assembly, and one of my strongest and happiest memories is of the Christingle services held there.'

1974-1999

Miss Birtill in the 1950s and 1960s had striven to establish the principle that Ockbrook was *one* school from infants to seniors, and that the normal assumption was that girls would progress from one section of the School to the next. By the later decades of the twentieth century, it had become more common for girls to leave at eleven or sixteen. The case for girls-only education at secondary level needs to be made forcibly; it is, as many will agree, a *very* strong case. Evidence from recent research shows that girls who have been educated in girls-only schools do significantly better when they get to university than those from co-educational establishments.

These were the issues which were very much in the mind of those running the School in the early 1990s. When Dr Rennie retired in August 1995, Miss Denise Patricia Bolland was appointed to take her place. She is a member of the religious Society of Friends (Quakers). In addition to her teaching qualifications in the sciences from the Universities of London and Surrey, she has a degree from the Open University and a master's degree in management from Brunel University. She came to Ockbrook with considerable senior management experience in both maintained and independent schools, most recently at Northwood College, a school belonging to the Girls' Schools Association.

With Miss Bolland's background in and enthusiasm for management and belief in team work it is not surprising that she has redeveloped the administration and 'marketing' of the School. Even more importantly, she has made effective learning an even greater priority. Every aspect of the School's provision (buildings, resources, policies and procedures) were reviewed and developed. In consequence, numbers overall increased by well over a hundred between 1995 and 1999. The composition of the staff changed: more full-time staff were employed. The retirement of respected and experienced

Miss Denise Bolland

teachers, which is always regretted, since the school inevitably becomes greatly indebted to them, enabled the appointment of younger highly qualified and experienced staff to create a healthy balance between young and old. Reports of formal official inspections have commended the excellence of the provision.

A great advantage and attraction of Ockbrook is its picturesque and historic setting, but parents look also for modern facilities for their children. Multiple use of the Birtill Hall for assemblies, music, drama and theatre, dance and physical education placed a heavy burden on the facilities. A sports hall had been needed for some years, and Miss Bolland persuaded the governors that the School should have one, and that it could be paid for. By 1998 the splendid complex was completed and in use. At the same time, a magnificent new grand piano was purchased to enhance the music provision, information technology facilities were extended and updated, and other plans are still under consideration.

Throughout the year 1999 the School celebrated its bicentenary with a whole series of sporting, cultural and social events. Highlights were a dance and drama production, 'A Journey Through Time Expressed in Six Themes', a festive musical concert, the Garden Party (enhanced, if that were possible, by excellent weather and followed by an old scholars' buffet supper), a production of 'My Fair Lady', a festival of net games for pupils, staff and former pupils, and the Bicentenary Sports Day. The culmination of the celebrations was the Bicentenary Service in Derby Cathedral on 23 September 1999, the actual date of the anniversary. The following evening four hundred guests gathered at Pride Park, Derby, for the Bicentenary Ball—a splendid occasion by any measure. On that occasion the Parents' Association presented the Head with a cheque for £20,000 for the School. The money had been raised at a variety of events throughout the year and after a great deal of endeavour. Then, to everyone's delight, the Lord Lieutenant of Derbyshire confirmed that HRH the Duchess of Gloucester would visit the School on 25 November. That really was the icing on the cake! At the end of 1999 Ockbrook School stands firmly and with great confidence as it moves into its third century.

1974-1999

HRH the Duchess of Gloucester at Ockbrook, 25 November 1999 (Derby Telegraph *picture*)

THE CAREERS and activities of Old Girls at the end of the 1990s are typified by the news sent in to the Association News Sheet for 1999. The details are for girls of all generations; as only sixty write of career as opposed to family information, the figures given here represent only an approximation to the real situation. However, there are some interesting features. A wide range of careers is represented. Doctors, dentists, medical researchers, nurses, midwives and therapists account for thirteen, maintaining the tradition of earlier eras. Education and child care accounts for ten: teachers of various types and specialisms, a nanny, and educational administrators. Some news is published of four at university, but two of these are studying part time as mature students, reflecting changes in society and the popularity of 'life-long education'. Two are working in the law. Writing, translating, art and design account for four. Three Old Girls work aboard aircraft as purser or stewardess. There is one in each of the following: theatre management, librarianship. sports administration, horticulture, hairdressing, chartered surveying, social administration and secretarial work. The new feature is the sixteen who are working in banking, commerce, retailing and business, including six who write enthusiastically about running their own or a family business.

As Ockbrook looks to the future, what can be foreseen? It is very dangerous to make prophecies. Elise Birtill wrote in 1950:

> I wonder what the year 2000 will see in Ockbrook? Some of you will undoubtedly live to re-visit Ockbrook in its bicentenary year. The promised hall will, perhaps, be mellow with age, and maybe we shall have more boarding accommodation, but I do not imagine our total numbers will be much above 220, which is the figure we are now nearing.

In no time at all Miss Birtill had proved herself thoroughly wrong: by the time she herself retired there were 300 pupils in the School. No-one foresaw the decline in demand for boarding. We shall therefore refrain from prophecy. Suffice it to say that, like a fine musical instrument, Ockbrook improves with age and becomes more flexible and responsive. Girls study new subjects and embrace new careers with enthusiasm.

Bishop Geoffrey Birtill, a former Chairman of Governors and a distant cousin of Miss Birtill, recently summarised the commitment of the Moravian Church to its schools in the following terms. They are a means of Christian outreach to the wider community. When they were opened to non-Moravians, just before the time Ockbrook was founded, they were never intended as sectarian or as a way of recruiting people into the Moravian Church specifically, but as a means of furthering a Christian approach to education and to the later life of their pupils. Moravian congregations have, in fact, often been enriched by the membership of former pupils and their families. The schools have therefore benefited both the Moravian and the wider Christian communities. It may be added that they have directly added to the richness of the whole of society by the continuing presence of a Christian ethos. The future success of Ockbrook School will depend not only on academic excellence, but on the survival of this commitment and of the notion of service to the wider community within a Christian context.

1999

Six girls were present when the Ladies' School at Ockbrook opened on 23 September 1799, and their names are to be found in Chapter 1. We list here the 491 girls and boys on the roll in July 1999. While most are from our own country, they come also from many other parts of the world.

ABBAS Reem
ADAMS Samantha
ALEMAYEHU Emelaf
ANDERSON Claire
ARMSTRONG Max
ASHCROFT Ria
ATKINSON Holly
ATTENBOROUGH Heidi
ATTER Jenna
BALL Charlotte
BALL Victoria
BARKER Lucy
BARNEY Claire
BARR John
BARTON Hollie
BARTON Victoria
BEASTALL Charlotte
BENTLEY-STEPHENS Alexandra
BICKLEY Madeleine
BLADEN Katharine
BOSTOCK Helen
BOWLEY Emma
BREWER Joanna
BRIGHOUSE Elizabeth
BRITTON Charlotte
BROUGHTON Annabel
BROWN Adonika
BROWN Emily
BROWN Lydia Rose
BUCKLE Robert
BURCHELL Ann-Marie
BUTLER Ellen
CHARLTON Rosie
CHURCHILL Helen
CLIFF Jasmin
CONSTABLE Jonathan
COX Michael

ACAR Claire
AINDOW Rebecca
ALEMAYEHU Nituh
ARMSTRONG Charlotte
ARMSTRONG Rebecca
ATKINSON Cherry Mae
ATTENBOROUGH Chloe
ATTENBOROUGH Katie
AUSTIN Bethany
BALL Felicity
BARKER Holly
BARKS Laura
BARNEY Louise
BARROWCLIFFE Rebecca
BARTON Richard
BAUGH Kirsty
BEAUMONT George
BHANOT Meenakshi
BLACKBURN Eleanor
BOS Anne
BOTTOMER Alexandra
BREWER Caroline
BRIGGS Shiarn
BRIGHOUSE Kathryn
BROOMHEAD Sarah
BROUGHTON Victoria
BROWN Amy
BROWN Henrietta
BROWN Rachael
BUCKLEY Harriet
BURNS-HOPKINS Kate
CALLADINE Joshua
CHIARELLA Megan
CLARKE Emily
CONSTABLE Emma
COX Isabelle
COX Richard

125

CRESSWELL Georgina	CUDWORTH Annabel
CUDWORTH Rebecca	DAHMANI Louisa
DALE Aimee	DALE Edward
DALE Jessica	DANN Helen
DAVIDSON Iona	DAVIS Rebecca
DAVIS Stefanie	DENNY Rebecca
DILKS Mijanou	DISNEY Jessica
DOHERTY Leah	DOLEMAN Alice F
DOWNES Sarah	DOWNES Simon
DRAYCOTT Amie	DUNDAS Jennifer
EARDLEY Rachel	EDEN Karyn
EDEN Kirstie	EDWARDS Rosemary
ELEY Gemma	ELEY Georgina
ELLABY-HOWARD Laura	ELLEN Katie
ELLIOTT Natalie	ELVIDGE Sarah
EVANS Freya	FALCONER Louise
FAULKNER Harriet	FAULKNER Naomi
FEARN Abbie	FEARN Matthew
FEDERICI Amelia	FEDERICI Francesca
FEDERICI Gabriella	FEDERICI Luke
FERGUSON Zella	FISHER Lucy
FLEMING Kathryn	FLINT Rebecca
FRAMPTON Christina	FREE Alexis
FRENCH Georgia	FUCHIWAKI Nao
FUCHIWAKI Yugo	GAJIC Natalya
GARSIDE Andrew	GARSIDE Heather
GAUBA Anmol	GEE Laura
GENEVER Isabella	GENEVER Joel
GENT Alexandra	GERGES Sandra
GERGES Sarah	GERGES Sylvia
GHUMAN Baljinder	GHUMAN Vicki
GIGG Sarah	GILL Samuel
GLAYSHER Georgiana	GOLDNEY Jennifer
GOLDNEY Michael	GORING Georgina
GOSNELL Sarah	GOSS Kym
GOTT Oliver	GOTT Samantha
GOURLAY Olivia	GREASLEY Emma
GURAM Rasneet	HADJIOSIF Felicity
HADJIOSIF Natalie	HAGUE Jennifer
HARRIS Tamsin	HARRISON Jacob
HARRISON Sophia	HASSALL Charlotte
HASSALL Elizabeth	HATTON Anthony
HATTON Megan	HAUXWELL Ruth
HAWKINS Eleanor	HAYLES Rebecca
HAYNES Carina	HAYNES Sarah

1999

HEADING Olivia
HEATH Luke
HELE Daryl
HENDERSON Kate
HENSHALL Katie
HILL Victoria
HODGSON Karis
HOLMES Jessica
HOLMES Natalie
HOOLEY Amy
HOUGH Ruth F
HUGHES April
HUNT Lucy
HYLAND Catherine
ICKE Sarah
JACKSON Jennifer
JACKSON Laura
JACOBS Roxi
JAMES Beth
JAMES Katie
JINKS Holly
JOHAL Sabrina
JOHANSSON Tim
JONES Emma
JONES Thomas
KEAVENEY Samuel
KELLY Isabelle
KEMP Suzi
KENT Harriet
KENYON Amelia
KENYON Jack
KIRK Felix
KIRK Pixie
KNOTT Katie
KONSTANTIS Thea
KOZLOWSKI-BEST Zachariah
KYTE Bethany
LAATS Christopher
LACEY Hannah
LAD Yasmin
LAKHANI Kishan
LANE Lloyd
LAST Abigail
LAST Rebecca
LEE Jessica

HEATH Esther
HELE Callam
HELLIWELL Petra
HENSHALL Gemma
HICKLING Louisa
HOBKINSON Emily
HOLMES Duncan
HOLMES Lucia
HOLMES Rebecca
HOPKINS Emily
HOWARD Samantha
HUNT Adam
HUTCHINSON Sarah
ICKE Lucy
JACKSON Hannah
JACKSON Laura
JACOBS Dannielle
JAKOBSEN (Kirk) Natalie
JAMES Grace
JENNINGS Kelly Anne
JOHAL Lydia
JOHANNSON Jessica
JOHNSON Danielle
JONES Jennifer
KAY Fenella
KEETLEY Rachel
KEMP Christie
KEMP Teri
KENT Thomas F
KENYON Charlotte
KENYON Sophie
KIRK Max
KIRK Skye
KONOWALIK Amy
KOZLOWSKA-BEST Rachel
KUMARI Tina
KYTE Emily
LAATS Gregory
LACEY Stephanie
LAKHANI Anjali
LAKIN Hannah
LANE Natalie
LAST Joshua
LEE Amy
LEEMING Georgia

LEEMING India
LIDDLE Tasmin
LLOYD Rhiannon
LORD Kate
LOWE Sarah
LOWNDES-TOOLE Alice
LYONS Emma
MACAULAY (Kirk) Kimberley
MACQUARRIE Beth
MALVENAN Dean
MALYSZ Victoria
MANSON Harriett
MARSHALL Lauren
MASON-GOODWIN Heather
McFARLAND Emma F
McILVENNA Emma
MENDLY Sarah
MERVIN Naomi
MILLER Laura
MITCHELL Caroline
MOLE Laura
MORGAN Christie
MORGAN Michael
MUIR Eileih
NEAL Caroline
NEWBOLD Grace
NG Hoi Ling (Anita)
NOBLE Laura
O'CONNOR Charlotte
OFFER Kirsty
O'SHEA-HERRIOT Helen
PALMER Edward
PALMER Shamus
PARROTT Leanne
PASSAM Laura
PATEL Shreena
PAVIS Matthew
PEARSON Alissa
PEARSON Laura
PENNY Jane
PEPPER Amy
PERKINS Cara
PIASKOWSKI Charlotte
PIDCOCK Charles
PILLAI Ashwini

LEWIN Isabelle
LLOYD Rebecca
LORD Jack
LORD Kim
LOWNDES Rebecca
LUKE Hannah
MACAULAY (Kirk) Joseph
MACH Loi
MALVENAN Clare
MALYSZ Carly
MANSFIELDMURPHY Charlotte
MARKWELL Claire
MASKALICK Hannah
MASON Lucy
McFARLAND Hannah
McILVENNA James
MERRITT Hannah
MILLER Kirsty
MILLETT Alexandra
MITCHELL Kara
MOORE Christopher
MORGAN Georgina
MRVIK Emma
NATH Nisha
NEWBOLD Alice
NEWPORT-BUTCHER Matia
NIX COLLINS Catherine
NOBLE Rebecca
O'CONNOR Laura
OLDFIELD Paige
O'SHEA-HERRIOT Hannah
PALMER Geordie
PARKES Rachel
PASS Lynsey
PATEL Nishal
PATTEN Katie
PEARSON Zoe
PEARSON Jennifer
PENDLETON Philippa
PENNY Rachel
PERKINS Alice
PERRY Isabel
PIASKOWSKI Sarah
PIGGOTT Grace
PILLAI Priya

1999

PIPONIDES Zoe	POPAT Sheena
PREECE Carley	PRICE Sally
PRIME Hayley	PRIME Michelle
PRIME Thomas	RANSOM Claire
RANSOM Sarah	REDGATE Georgina
REES Anna	REES Helen
REGAN Claire	RICHARDSON Elizabeth
RIGLEY-WILLIAMSON Fiona	RIVERS Hannah
RIVERS Rachel	ROBERTS Maura
ROBERTS Grace	ROBERTS Nia
ROSS Alexander	ROSS Esme
ROSS Sarah	RUDD Lexie
SANDHU Kaljinder	SANDHU Parminder
SANDHU Priya	SANTON Harriet
SCALES Katie	SEABRIDGE George
SEDGWICK Daniel	SHARMA Priti
SHAW Ashley	SHED Rachael
SHEEHY-SMITH Eleanor-Jane	SHEPHERD Caroline
SHEPPARD Joseph	SHUTTLEWORTH Alice
SHUTTLEWORTH Matthew	SIMMS Sarah
SIMONET Annaelle	SIMONET Fanch
SIMPSON Whitney	SLACK Adam
SLACK Joseph	SLACK Oliver
SLACK Thomas	SMALLWOOD Rachel
SMEDLEY Cyd	SMITH Benjamin
SMITH Charlotte	SMITH Chloe
SMITH Emily	SMITH Hayley SMITH Holly
SMITH Jessica	SMITH Joshua
SMITH Lauren	SMITH Lucy
SMITH Nichola	SMITH Victoria
SOLLOWAY Bethan	SPENSER William
SPRAKES Alison	SPRINGTHORPE Rebecca
SPRINGTHORPE Sarah	STANFIELD Chelsey
STENNER Claudia	STEVENSON Melissa
STIMPSON Gemma	STOREY Annie
STOTT Michaela	STOTT Stephanie
STREET Daniel	STREET Rebekah
STRETTON Caroline	STRETTON Hannah
SUMMERS Charlotte	SUMMERS Natalie
SUMMERSCALES Charlotte	SUMMERSCALES Emma
SUMMERSCALES Thomas	SURTEES Alexandra
SUTTON Georgina	SUTTON Samantha
SZWEC Victoria	TAMS Rosie
TAYLOR Leanne	THOMPSON Caroline
THOMPSON Charlotte	THOMPSON Emma

THORNE Jonathan
THORPE Jessica
THORPE Nicola
TOMLINSON Christopher
TOMLINSON Laura
TORKONIAK Mykola
TOWLER Kathryn
TREVOR Chantalle
TUCKER Elaine
TURNER Jacqui
TYLER Max
VAUGHAN Jennifer
WAHEDNA Natasha
WALKER Ashley
WALKER Jennifer
WARDLE Rebecca
WEST Emily
WESTWOOD Lyndsey
WHITE Victoria
WHITTINGTON Samuel
WILSON Heather
WILSON Lydia
WILSON Rosemary
WITHEY Stephanie
WOOD Rachel
WOODCOCK Claire
WRZESINSKI Leanne

THORNE Katherine
THORPE Michael
THORPE Yasmin
TOMLINSON Emma
TOMLINSON Lucy
TOWLER John
TREVOR Alexis
TRIVETT Emily
TUCKER Laura
TYLER Eleanor
UREN Molly
VESSE Rachel
WAHEDNA Sara
WALKER Hollie
WARDLE Oliver
WEIGHTMAN Katie
WESTWOOD Anne
WHITE Serena
WHITING Alexandra
WILLIAMS Alexandra
WILSON Jessica
WILSON Rosanna
WINDLE Nicole
WOOD Lyndsey
WOOD Shirleena
WORRALL Samantha
WRZESINSKI Natasha

Teachers at Ockbrook School since 1799

School records do not make it possible to compile a complete list: names or initials are often not given and the term of service of the teacher concerned is not always clearly recorded. Dates given here mean simply that the teacher was known to be active on the date or dates stated. Part-time and temporary teachers have mostly been omitted from this list.

Anna Pogson
 (governess) 1799-1802
Elizabeth Sulger
 (governess) 1802-08
[Sr] Cox 1808
Ann Templeton 1808-17
 (governess)
Margaret Collis 1813-16
Agnes LaTrobe 1816
Mary Ody (governess) 1817-18
Frances Bendall 1818-21(?)
 (governess)
Sarah Ferris 1823
Mary Jones 1824
Hannah Clarke 1824
Eliza Clarke 1824
A Jackson 1826
Sarah Church
 (governess) 1828 (or earlier)-34
[Sr] Becker 1831
Harriet Montgomery 1834
[Sr] Murch 1834
Mary Birtill (temp.) 1834
Catherine Waiblinger
 (governess) 1834-44
Janetta Fuller 1841-43
Susannah Robinson
 (governess) 1844-73
Matilda Gregor 1851-73
Elizabeth Oaks 1851
Mary Alice Bayne 1853
Ellen Bush 1848-61
Margaret Craig 1861
Anna Beckman 1861-62

[Sr] Winck 1862
[Sr] Bohe 1863
[Sr] Redford 1863
H Harvey 1863
M A Kaltofen 1863
Sarah Humberstone 1863
[Sr] Wuster
[Sr] Ellmore
Lydia Liley (principal) 1873-74
Agnes Robinson 1871
Johanna Machtler 1871
Jessie Buicke 1871
Eleanor Osborne
 (principal) 1874-89
Florence Holmes 1878
Emma Lang 1881
Eleanor Lang 1881
[Miss] Walker
Susanna Boag 1881
Martha Keuge 1881
Eliza Hanna 1881
Matilda Barnes 1881
Mary Harvey
 (principal) 1889-1914
Sophia L Herzberger 1891
Mary Rea 1891
Sarah L Hanna 1891
[Miss] Kirkland 1896-1901
A Cade 1898-1901
H von Flotow 1901-10
J E Shawe 1901
[Miss] Reeves 1902-05
[Miss] Corney 1902-11
Charlotte M. Nelson c.1920

[Miss] Mellowes 1902
[Miss] Birgfeld 1902
[Miss] Ellis 1902
[Miss] Libbey 1902
[Miss] Dingemans 1902
[Miss] Garve 1902
L Hanna 1903
C Dawes 1903
E M Stokes 1903-12
[Miss] Hewson 1903-12
[Miss] Barker 1906
[Miss] Piercy 1910-12
[Miss] King 1912-14
Ellen Irene Low (1912-62)
[Miss] Ward 1912-
[Miss] Davies
E Elizabeth Titterington MA (head) 1914-1926
Jessie F Orr BA (deputy, later head) 1918-45
[Miss] Nicholson 1914-
[Miss] Boden 1920-38
[Miss] Gunston 1922
[Miss] Buckland 1923-26
[Miss] Garratt 1923
[Miss] Smith 1923
[Miss] Heyes BSc 1923-27
[Miss] Harris 1923
[Miss] Westall LLB 1926-?30
[Miss] Axtell 1926-29
[Miss] Hyde BSc 1927
[Miss] Emery 1929-37
[Miss] Drummond 1930-31
[Miss] Hyde 1930-35
Madge Poole 1930-35
[Miss] Ragg 1930
[Miss] Wood 1930-38
[Miss] Christie MA 1932
Margaret Wood 1933-39
G M Harris BSc 1935-62
Dora Blue BA (Mrs Condy) 1935-41
Christine Andrews (Mrs Lawley) 1937
[Miss] Frankland 1937-38

[Miss] Radford 1937
[Miss] Bellamy 1937
[Miss] Bayne 1938
A M Jones BSc
M Elise Birtill MA (head) 1945-70
D Pilling (née Boyd) 1939-72
[Miss] Talbot 1940
[Miss] Richardson 1941
F M Hutchinson 1951
H M Johnson 1951-55
Lois E Parish 1938-68
[Miss] Brewster 1945-50
M J Randall 1951-53
P Shephard 1951-55
I E Twidell 1951
J P Whalley 1951
[Miss] Middleton 1955
B E H Bell BA 1953-58 and senior mistress 1964-74
[Miss] Palmer 1955
[Miss] Jessop 1954
[Miss] Kimmins 1953
B. Holmes 1956-58
[Miss] Fagg 1959
[Miss] Gilligan 1958
[Miss] Felix-Williams 1957
[Miss] M Lowe 1957-
[Miss] Dempster 1957-
Vera N Fisher 1957
Joan G Jones 1957-
A Vaughan (née Lester) 1947-48, 1957-65
Dorothy Ward 1957-59
[Miss] Owen 1958
D. Challis 1960
[Miss] Corbett 1963-69
[Miss] Mills 1965
[Miss] Salt 1966
[Miss] Jenkins 1966
Mr L S Harrison BA 1966-71
[Miss] Browne 1966
[Miss] Quinn 1966-67
[Miss] Beard 1967
[Miss] Murray-Smith 1967
[Miss] Watch 1967

Teachers 1799-1999

[Miss] Hamilton 1967
K. R. Irving 1968
A. Giggs 1968-69
A. Glazebrook 1968
S. L. Thomas 1968
R. M. Weir 1968
[Miss] Jordison 1969
[Miss] Hudson 1969
[Miss] Weber 1969
A J Lewis MA PhD (head) 1970-74
J B Allen 1976-79
C C Barrett MA 1969-86
D M Borsley 1971
V Carlisle BA 1976-88
M E Cawson 1971-81
J Clark 1971-95
P Daniels 1965-85
D M Enion BA 1975-77
E Fitton BSc 1956-84
J Glover BSc 1971-81
L Griffith 1976
C Hallett BSc 1976
C Philps 1977-70
G Campion 1973-75
Mr J C Hawkins BSc 1971-90
E Hayes MA 1976
A M Hope BA PhD 1971
P Howarth 1971-76
E Horobin LRAM 1976-81
A E Illingworth BA 1971-76
K R Irving BSc 1971
S W Jagg 1971-76
G Johnson 1971-76
R D Jones BA 1969-76
J M Knibbs BSc 1971
J S Litchfield 1976-81
K Little BA 1974-95
J Lowes BSc 1971-82
E R Madaras BA 1971
M E A Marshall BA 1969-85
  (sen. mistress)
A Nixon BA 1971
B M Pemberton BA 1971
M H Sanders 1976
A Stewart MA BMus 1976

J I Smith BSc 1971-76
C F Strong BSc 1976-81
S L Stober BA 1971
M Taylor BSc
C Titley (Horobin) NNEB 1967-98
R M Weir BA 1971
S W White BA 1971
M L Wood 1976
J Wozencroft 1976
A Beryl Driver BA (head) 1974-86
J H Biss BA 1980-
M F Borgeat BA 1978-81
V Kingsbury 1977-80
H Fairclough 1978-80
D S Footer BA 1980-84
J Halliday 1981-84
D E Harris BA 1981
H Hawkings BSc 1981
S Heathcote BA 1977-96
A Logie BA 1979-
K E Newton BA 1981-87
O E R Peutrell 1977-94
S E Smith BSc 1980-
S Stubley 1981
C J Westland 1979-88
D A Wilkinson BSc 1980-82
P D Yates 1977-88
A. Beardsley 1982-99
K Onesti 1984-94
R Ledbury 1984-96
H Jameson 1986-96
J Ash BA (deputy head) 1992-97
J Gwatkin Cert. Ed. 1989-
N Byron BA MEd (acting head
  1986-87) on staff 1984-90
A White 1985-92
Myra Rennie BSc PhD
  (head) 1987-95
M Barker 1988-97
K Murdoch 1993-95
Denise P Bolland BA MSc
  (head 1995-)
J Thwaites 1995-97
H Peachey BA 1997-98
S Chamberlain, BA MA 1987-99

Mr A Clegg BSc 1995-98
S Crompton BEd 1994-
K Hawkins Cert. Ed. 1988-
S Jones (Taylor) BA
H Killip BEd 1996-98
C Lafferty BEd 1995-
I Mellors 1992-
S Wright BSc 1992-
Mr J Hampton 1996-97
E S Berry BEd 1995-
M Burton BA 1998
C Chivers BEd 1997-99
A Kent BSc 1987-
E S Newton BEd 1992-
P A Parker Cert. Ed. 1989-
L Rigley BA 1992-99
Mr J Robertson BA 1995-
L J Shaw Dip PE 1984-
S Taylor BA 1994-
A Tooley BA 1996-
S E Turner BSc PhD 1994-99
G A Veasey Cert. Ed. 1992-99
Mr D Williams BEd 1996-
C L Brown BA 1986-99

J Brown BSc 1990-
J G Cockle BA MA 1987-
E Dunford BSc 1996-
Mr M. Harrison 1990-95
Mr H. Holden 1983-90
C Caulton 1997
F Faulkner BSc MA 1995
E A Hoyle BA 1985-
A Jablonski MA 1981-
A Jamieson BEd 1998-
E L Jones BEd 1989-
F McCreddin BA 1994-
Mr G Maskalick BA MA 1997-
S Mitchell BA 1992-
J Mullineaux BEd 1999-
Y Oakes BA LLAM ALAM 1985-
M I Owen-Jones RSA 1992
A Renow BA MEd 1996-
M Smith BA MA 1997-
S Throssell BSc 1993-
P Wakeman BA 1998-
H P Ward BA MEd PhD 1988-
M Watkins BA 1997-

BIBLIOGRAPHY

Books, pamphlets, articles and printed documents

Anon. *An Outline of Moravian History*, undated pamphlet, no place of publication
Anon. 'How the Moravians became an educational church', *Moravian Almanack and Yearbook*, 1872, 92-98
Anon. 'Introducing Ockbrook School', *Moravian Messenger*, Oct. 1957, 13-16
Anon. 'New Extensions—and Unity', *Moravian Messenger*, Feb. 1965, 33-35
Anon. 'Ockbrook head is Retiring After 25 Years', *Derby Evening Telegraph*, 4 July 1970, 5
Anon. 'Ockbrook School Speech Day', *Derby Evening Telegraph*, 25 July 1941, 9 col 3
Anon. 'Report of the Provincial Synod of 1853', *Fraternal Messenger*, 1853, 21-22
Anon. 'Sr Jessie Farquhar Orr', [obituary] *Moravian Messenger*, September 1957, 7
Anon. *Village Trails 3 - in Erewash. Ockbrook.* Erewash Borough Council: Long Eaton, 1984; also 1992
An Old Pupil, 'The late Miss Mary Harvey', *Moravian Messenger*, 1932, 76
Birtill, G., 'Arthur James Lewis, M.A., D.D. June 29, 1914 - June 20, 1990', *Moravian Messenger*, September 1990, 163-167
Birtill, G., 'The Gift of Happiness. Appreciation of Sr Beryl Driver, Headmistress of Ockbrook School 1974-1986', *Moravian Messenger*, May 1987, 85-86
Birtill, G., 'New Head of Ockbrook School [Dr Myra Rennie]', *Moravian Messenger*, May 1987, 86-87
Birtill, M. E., 'The Girls' School', *Moravian Messenger*, July 1961, 15-18
Birtill, M. E., 'Ockbrook School', *Derbyshire Countryside*, v. 19 no. 4, 1952, 85-86 & 99
Borer, M. C., *Willingly to School*, Guildford and London: Lutterworth Press, 1976

Bulmore, Barbara M., *Moravian Education at Fulneck Schools, Yorkshire, in the Eighteenth and Nineteenth Centuries*. PhD thesis, University of Manchester, 1992

Cooper, Joan, 'The Moravian contribution to higher education in the British Isles', *Moravian Messenger*, 1937, July, 79-80; August, 89; September, 107-109

Davis, R., *The Grammar School*, Harmondsworth: Penguin, 1967

Hinchliffe, G., 'Teacher of Nations. Some educational ideas of John Amos Comenius', *Soviet Education Study Bulletin*, vol. 10, 1992, no. 2, 38-40

House of Commons, 'Ockbrook' in *Population. Comparative Account of the Population of Great Britain in the Years 1801, 1811, 1821 and 1831*, London, 1831

Inchley, A., '162-year-old School Looks Ahead', *Derby Evening Telegraph*, 8 June 1961, 22

Johnson, Marion, *Memories of Ockbrook and Borrowash*, Ockbrook/Borrowash, 1990

Johnson, Marion, *Ockbrook and its Parson, Samuel Hay 1810-1852*, Borrowash: Greenway, 1991

Johnson, Marion, *Ockbrook in the 1820s*, Ockbrook and Erewash Local History Series no. 4, 1991

King, E. and Nelson, C. M., *The Brethren's Unity or 'Moravians' in Ockbrook 1750-1950*, Ockbrook, 1950

Leibert, M. W., [Bishop], 'The Status of Moravian schools at home and abroad', *Moravian Messenger*, vol. xxi (15), 1911, 226-228

Lewis, A. J. *Zinzendorf the Ecumenical Pioneer*, Philadelphia: Westminster Press, 1962 (esp. 171-176)

Low, Ellen Irene, *1912-1962. Fifty Years at Ockbrook School*, [self-published], 18 pp., photograph, 1962

McGibbon, A. and Linyard, F., *Ockbrook Moravian Church and Settlement 1750-1975*, 16 pp. pamphlet, Ockbrook, 1975

Meynell, R., 'Notes and Queries: Ockbrook's Moravian School', *Derbyshire Advertiser*, 2 August 1957, 11, cols 3-6

Montgomery, R. J., *Examinations. An Account of their Evolution as Administrative Devices in England*, London: Longmans, Green, 1965, esp. 48-51

Murphy, D., *Comenius*, Dublin: Irish Academic Press, 1995.

M.Y., 'Onerous duty of independent schools. Ockbrook School's 150th birthday gala', *Moravian Messenger*, Sept. 1949, 137-138; and 'Schools can teach standards. Ockbrook Girls' School Speech Day', the same, 138-139

Roach, John, *Public Examinations in England 1850-1900*, Cambridge: Cambridge University Press, 1971

Sadler, Michael, *Report on Secondary and Higher Education in Derbyshire*, Derby, London and Watford: Administrative

Bibliography

County of Derby Education Committee, 1905
Sadler, Sir Michael, 'The scholarship system in England to 1890 and some of its developments', in Sadler, M. et al., *Essays on Examinations*, London: Macmillan, 1936, 1-78
Sample, E., 'Ockbrook School', *Derbyshire Life and Countryside*, v. 30. n. 10, Oct. 1965, 26-28
Sharp, P. and Dunford, J., 'The development of the education service in the nineteenth and twentieth centuries', in Sharp and Dunford, *The Education System in England and Wales*, London and New York: Longman, 1990, 1-25
Strong, Ruth, *A History of Fulneck Girls' School 1741-1994*, Pudsey: Fulneck School, 1995
Topham, Anne, *Memories of the Kaiser's Court*, London: Methuen 1914
Tyndale, Mrs T. G., *Selections from the Correspondence of Mrs Ely Bates [Bates, Elizabeth M.] and Incidents from her Early Life*, 2 vols, Oxford: Henry Alden, 1872, 1873
Walder, Ernest [authorship assumed], 'Ockbrook Schools', *Moravian Missions*, April 1911, 70-72
Whyatt, D., 'Ockbrook School', *Derbyshire Life and Countryside*, 1986, v. 51. n. 6, 42-43

School Magazines, Prospectuses, etc.

The New S.T.A.R.: School of Thought and Reading; Striving to Attain Renown, [mimeographed], Ockbrook Ladies' School 1901-1908
Ockbrook Girls' School Magazine, [printed], July 1909-December 1914 (nos 1-12; described as 'New Series' from no. 5 onwards)
Ockbrook Girls' School 1799 to 1961 Building Appeal Fund [brochure]
Ockbrook School Notice to Parents, June 1953 [printed pamphlet]
Ockbrook School Magazine, 1921-75 (nos 13-75, New series); April 1984, 1977-1978, 1988-1980, 1988-89, 1989-1990. The 1977-1978 issue is entitled simply *Ockbrook Girls' School*, and the 1978-1980 issue *Ockbrook School*.
Ockbrook School [Prospectuses], c. 1968, 1973, 1975
'Ockbrook School, Derby'. Entries in *The Girls' School Yearbook*, 1966, 1971, 1981

Local and Public Records

In the Derbyshire Record Office, Matlock:

'An Account of the Ages of all persons, including children of whatever age in the Parish of Ockbrook taken May 28, 29 and 30 1821 by

James Morley Churchwarden and William Winterton Acting Overseer of the Poor': MS document.

'An Assessment of ten pence in the pound to be levied on the Parish of Ockbrook in the County of Derby for the Maintenance of the Poor': MS document in which the space for overseers' and church wardens' names is left blank; signed at end 'G. Cumming, Sept. 1826'

Education Committee Minutes: Minutes of the Finance and General Purposes Sub-committee, 1918-1919, esp. 31 Dec. 1918

'Ockbrook Valuation, 1828': leather-bound MS volume, accompanied by a large map on which all sites are numbered in agreement with the entries in the book

In the Ockbrook Moravian Church Archives:

Burial records
Community Diary
Diary of the Single Sisters
Elders' Conference Minutes
Extracts from the Survey of the Liberty of Ockbrook, relating to the Moravian Settlement [1826]. Copied 9 Mar. 1931 by Rev. F. E. Birtill: MS document
Girls' School Cash Books
Lebenslauf of Anna Pogson [MS document]
Memorabilia of the Congregation
Miscellaneous documents and correspondence
Resolutions of the Synod of the Protestant Church of the United Brethren assembled at Herrnhut in the Year 1789, Chapter VIII: Of the Education of Children
Moravian periodicals: The *Messenger* and *Moravian Messenger*

In the Ockbrook School archive collection

The School collection is not a systematic archive, and few records have been preserved. Photographs from Miss Osborne's period as Head (1874ff.) onwards are of visual interest. A 16mm. film of the daily life of the School, made in 1949, also survives and has been converted to videotape. The following items form almost the sum total of the written and printed records.

Log Book 1930-37
Head Girls' Diary 1971-1984. MS notebook
School Prospectuses for c.1968-1975
Notebooks containing names, dates of birth and health records (height, weight, etc) of pupils, dated 1920-30, 1925, Jan. 1931-July 1936, 1936-41, 1941-44, 1944[-47],

Bibliography

1949-, Sept. 1950[-1966], 1954, 1956-59, 1959-62, 1962-66, 1966-74
Notebook containing domestic staff wages, 1909-1942
Charts and diagrams [produced by pupils as a project?] showing
    (1) age of the buildings in Ockbrook village
    (2) plan of the School buildings in order of acquisition/ construction
    (3) growth of the School, boarders and day pupils 1920-1975
Attendance registers, miscellaneous, dated 1953-69; 1958-70; 1955-70; 1960s; from 1971
Album with Ockbrook School Music Society programmes
Miscellaneous newspaper cuttings

In the National Archives at Moravian Church House

Correspondence, governors' minutes and unpublished reports and other documents, c.1944-1967
Moravian Almanack and Yearbook, c.1870-1880
'The Place of Ockbrook Girls' School in the National Education System'. [Confidential typewritten document prepared in response to the Fleming Report and supplied to the Governors; dated October 1944]

In the University of Nottingham East Midlands Collection

Census returns for 1841, 1851, 1861, 1871, 1881 and 1891 (microform)

In the University of Nottingham Library

Nottingham Journal, 21 and 28 September 1799
    (weekly broadsheet newspaper)
Nottingham Review and General Advertiser for the Midland Counties, Friday, March 21, 1817, p. 3, col. 4

From the Public Record Office at Kew:

'1920 Ockbrook School Full Inspection', doc. no. ED 109/749
'1924 Ockbrook School Supplementary', doc. no. ED 109/750
'1930 Ockbrook School Full Inspection', doc. no. ED 109/751
'1950-51 Ockbrook School', doc. no. ED 109/8708

Directories in chronological order

Pigot and Co's *Directory for Derbyshire*, 1828, 1831, 1835 and 1841
History, Gazetteer and Directory of Derbyshire by Samuel Bagshaw 1846

Bibliography

Post Office Directory 1848. Derbyshire. Also the equivalent volumes for 1855, 1864 and 1876
Pigot's *Directory for Derbyshire*, 1850
Slater's *Derbyshire Directory*, 1850
History, Gazetteer and Directory of the County of Derby, by Francis White and Co., 1857
Harrod & Co.'s *Postal and Commercial Directory of Derbyshire*, 1870
Wright's Directory of Derby, 1871
Derbyshire Red Book, Almanack, Diary and Annual Register, Bemrose, 1873
C. N. Wright's *Directory of S. Derbyshire*, Bemrose, 1874
History, Topography and Directory of Derbyshire, by T. Bulmer & Co., c. 1894
History, Topography and Directory of Derbyshire, Nottinghamshire, Leicester and Rutland, by T. Bulmer and Co., 1895
Kelly's Directory of Derbyshire, Kelly, 1895; 1899; 1912 and 1922